little & LARGE
sticker activity book

VIKINGS

Miles Kelly
PUBLISHING

First published in 2006 by Miles Kelly Publishing Ltd
Bardfield Centre, Great Bardfield, Essex, CM7 4SL

This edition printed in 2008

2 4 6 8 10 9 7 5 3

Editorial Director: Belinda Gallagher

Art Director: Jo Brewer

Assistant Editors: Amanda Askew, Hannah Todd

Cover Designer: Tom Slemmings

Reprographics: Anthony Cambray, Mike Coupe, Stephan Davis, Ian Paulyn

Production Manager: Elizabeth Brunwin

British Library Cataloguing-in-Publication Data
A catalogue record for this book is available from the British Library

ISBN 978-1-84236-668-4

Printed in China

All photographs and artworks are from MKP archives

www.mileskelly.net
info@mileskelly.net

www.factsforprojects.com

Introduction

The Vikings lived in Scandinavia over 1000 years ago. Viking warriors were famous for their bravery and violence. They battled to win new lands and gradually spread through Europe.

Viking explorers travelled far and wide, and set up new villages in Iceland, Greenland and Russia. They were the very first people from Europe to discover North America in AD 1000.

With this great sticker book you can learn all about life as a Viking. Discover which king was famous for his cruelty and how Vikings settled arguments. Then impress your friends with amazing facts!

Mini stickers!

Who were the great Viking warriors? How did Vikings bathe? Which stories did Vikings like to tell? Use your mini stickers to learn all about Vikings and their daily life.

Battles and warriors – Vikings were famous for their bravery

Kings – At the head of Viking society were kings or chiefs

Viking life – In their spare time Vikings relaxed with games and sports

Gods – Vikings worshipped many different gods and goddesses

Legends – Vikings loved telling exciting stories and hearing about magical tales

Battles and warriors

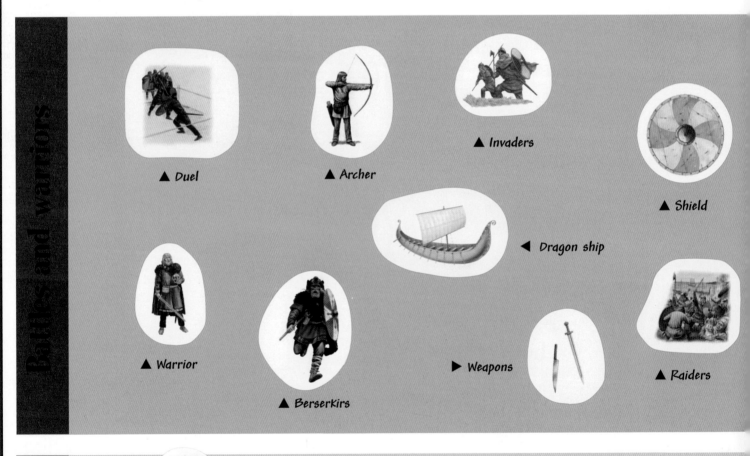

▲ Duel

▲ Archer

▲ Invaders

▲ Shield

◀ Dragon ship

▲ Warrior

▲ Berserkirs

▶ Weapons

▲ Raiders

Kings

▲ Erik Bloodaxe

▲ King Cnut

▲ Sigurd the Stout

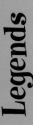

Viking life

▲ Farming

▲ Pots

▼ Mealtime

▲ Making clothes

▲ Feeding chickens

◄ Games

▲ Longhouse

▲ Toilet

▲ Boys playing

▼ Mother and child

▲ Sauna

Gods

▲ Freyja

◄ Odin

► Thor

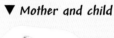

▲ Tyr

▲ Njord

Legends

▲ Lucky charm

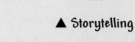

▲ Storytelling

► Ragnarok

◄ Valkyrie

Life as a Viking

  ▶ Duel

Viking warriors challenged people who insulted them, or their families, to a deadly duel

▶ Lucky charm

This is a Viking lucky charm that is shaped like Thor's hammer

 ▶ Weapons

Many warriors gave their swords names as they were their most treasured possession

◀ Freyja

The Viking goddess Freyja rode in a chariot pulled by cats

 ▶ Sigurd the Stout

Sigurd the Stout believed that whoever carried his flag was sure of victory for his army – but would die himself

 ▼ Archer

Viking archers used bows made of yew wood and twisted plant fibres

◀ Pots

Vikings used pots made from pottery and silver for cooking, and drank from hollowed-out cattle horns

 ▶ Longhouse

Viking longhouses were large enough for the family's animals to live in too

KEY:

Battles and warriors

Kings

Viking life

Gods

Legends

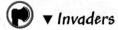 ▼ **Invaders**

Vikings invaded new lands and made settlements, and claimed the land for their own

 ▲ **Farming**

The Vikings realized that the British Isles provided good farmland and safe areas to live

◄ **Shield**

This round shield is made of wood and covered with leather

 ► **Sauna**

Vikings bathed in clouds of steam– very similar to saunas– which are still popular today

◄ **Odin**

Odin was the Viking god of war – he rode an eight-legged horse

 ▼ **Warrior**

Viking warriors were famous for their bravery and violence

▼ **Games**

This board and counters were probably used to play the game 'hneftafl' – which is like chess

▼ **Ragnarok**

Viking legends told stories of how the world was going to end – at the battle of Ragnarok

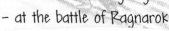

Many Viking rulers had strange or violent names, such as Svein Forkbeard, Thorfinn Skullsplitter and Sigurd the Stout.

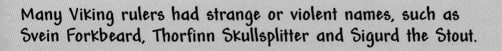

Viking vessels

Vikings were brave adventurers who were keen to seek out new lands. Viking longboats were fast and could travel far across open seas. They were made from long planks fitted onto wooden frames. Vikings carefully watched and kept note of the position of the stars and Sun to navigate (find their way) at sea. Viking explorers used these longboats to reach America about 1000 years ago.

Sails were invented at least 5000 years ago. Vikings used both sails and oars – this helped them to travel quickly.

Vikings

▲ Duel

▲ Archer

▲ Weapons

▲ Sigurd the Stout

▲ Pots

▲ Longhouse

▲ Lucky charm

▲ Freyja

▶ Archer

▲ Duel

◀ Weapons

▲ Sigurd the Stout

▲ Pots

◀ Longhouse

▶ Lucky charm

▲ Freyja

Vikings

◄ Invaders

▲ Farming

► Warrior

► Shield

◄ Games

► Sauna

▼ Odin

▼ Ragnarok

▲ Invaders

▲ Shield

▲ Warrior

▲ Farming

▲ Games

▲ Sauna

▲ Odin

▲ Ragnarok

◄ Berserkirs

▼ Making clothes

► Erik Bloodaxe

▼ Feeding chickens

▲ Mother and child

◄ Toilet

▼ Valkyrie

► Tyr

▲ Berserkirs

▲ Making clothes

▲ Erik Bloodaxe

▲ Feeding chickens

▲ Mother and child

▲ Toilet

▲ Tyr

▲ Valkyrie

Vikings

▼ King Cnut

▲ Dragon ship

▲ Raiders

▼ Boys playing

▲ Mealtime

► Thor

▼ Njord

▲ Storytelling

Deadly duel!

Vikings followed a strict code of honour. Men and women were dignified and proud, and honour was very important to them. It was a disgrace to be called a cheat or a coward, or to run away from a fight. Vikings also prized loyalty. They swore solemn promises to be faithful to lords and comrades and sealed bargains by shaking hands.

Make a Viking pendant

You will need:
- string • modelling clay
- white and yellow paint • paintbrush

1. Shape some animal fangs from modelling clay.
2. Make a hole at the widest part of the fang.
3. Paint the fangs white and yellow.
4. Thread string through the fangs and wear around your neck

Quarrels between Viking families led to feuds. These could continue for many months, with many people on both sides being killed.

Life as a Viking

 ◄ **Berserkirs**
Berserkir warriors rushed madly into battle–wearing animal skins and chain-mail armour

◄ **Making clothes**
Viking women spun sheep's wool and wove it into warm cloth on tall, upright looms

► **Erik Bloodaxe**
Erik Bloodaxe was famous for his cruelty – he was the last Viking to rule north-east England

 ▼ **Feeding chickens**
Feeding chickens was work for Viking girls – they learnt how to grow vegetables and cook by helping their mother

▲ **Tyr**
Tyr was a fierce god who Vikings asked to help them win victories

▲ **Toilet**
Viking toilets may have looked like this – they used dry moss, grass or leaves as toilet paper

► **Mother and child**
Viking women made important household decisions, cooked, cleaned, made clothes and raised the children

▲ **Valkyrie**
Vikings believed that Valkyries were wild warrior women who carried men who had died in battle to live with Odin in the hall of the brave dead

KEY:

 Battles and warriors

 Kings

 Viking life

 Gods

 Legends

▼ Dragon ship

Viking dragon ships were long and sleek, made from overlapping planks of wood, held together with iron nails

▲ Storytelling

Vikings loved telling each other sagas – stories that recorded past events and famous people's lives

▼ Raiders

Loyal warriors were sent on journeys – they sailed away from their homes to attack villages so that they could steal their valuables

▶ King Cnut

King Cnut ruled a large empire but didn't want to look too proud, so he tried to control the sea, even though he knew he would fail

▶ Thor

Vikings believed that Thor was the god of storms and that he could control the Universe with his hammer

◀ Boys playing

Viking boys practised fighting with swords made from wood and small, light shields

▶ Njord

Vikings believed that Njord was the god of the sea – he married the giantess, Skadi, who watched over mountains

▲ Mealtime

Viking women and slaves cooked huge meals over open fires – and served them to feasting warriors

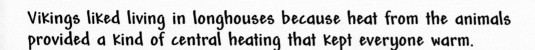

Vikings liked living in longhouses because heat from the animals provided a kind of central heating that kept everyone warm.

Victorious Vikings!

Read on to find out about some ancient record-breaking facts

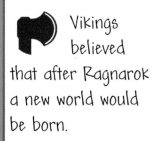

Vikings believed that after Ragnarok a new world would be born.

Viking longhouses were usually built on sloping ground so that animal waste ran down the hill!

If a Viking man wanted to marry he had to ask the woman's father for permission – if permission was granted the marriage would go ahead.

• Each Viking soldier had to provide his own weapons and armour. Wealthy Vikings could afford metal helmets and tunics, and sharp swords.

• Vikings made long journeys across land in winter because the frozen ground was easier to walk across with heavy loads.

• Every year Vikings met at the Thing. This was an open-air assembly of all men in the area. It met to punish criminals and make new laws.

Viking men wore make-up! They particularly liked eyeliner – probably made from soot.

Discover more interesting facts about Vikings

• The Vikings believed that runes – their way of writing – had magic healing powers. Runes were written on women's palms during childbirth to protect them from pain.

• Viking men and women liked to wear brightly patterned clothes. They often decorated their clothes with strips of woven braid.

• Viking children did not go to school. Daughters helped their mothers with cooking and cleaning, fed farm animals, and learned to spin, weave and sew. Sons helped their fathers in the workshop or on the farm.

Vikings believed that two ravens called Thought and Memory flew alongside Odin – the god of war.

Viking men and women wore lots of jewellery, partly to show how wealthy they were.

If a Viking was injured in the stomach, then he was made to eat onions. If his comrades could smell onions from his wound they knew it was bad!

The Vikings imported boatloads of broken glass from Germany, to melt into beautiful glass beads.

Fun facts

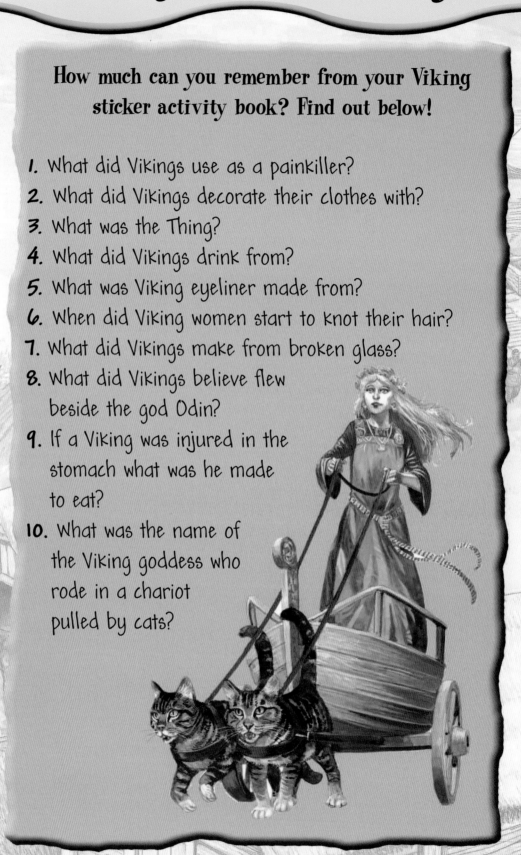

Berserkir warriors rushed madly into battle, chewing their shields and growling like wolves – this was done to scare enemies.

Viking warriors' swords were their most treasured possession – they would sometimes even give them a special name!

Vikings loved riddles and even liked to play practical jokes on each other.

Test your memory!

How much can you remember from your Viking sticker activity book? Find out below!

1. What did Vikings use as a painkiller?
2. What did Vikings decorate their clothes with?
3. What was the Thing?
4. What did Vikings drink from?
5. What was Viking eyeliner made from?
6. When did Viking women start to knot their hair?
7. What did Vikings make from broken glass?
8. What did Vikings believe flew beside the god Odin?
9. If a Viking was injured in the stomach what was he made to eat?
10. What was the name of the Viking goddess who rode in a chariot pulled by cats?

Viking women went to war but they did not fight! Instead, they nursed wounded warriors and cooked meals for hungry soldiers.

11. What did Sigurd the Stout believe would happen to anyone who carried his flag?
12. What was the name of the Viking god of war?
13. What did Vikings call the end of the world?
14. What did the god Odin ride on?
15. Vikings bathed in clouds of what?
16. What did Vikings believe the Valkyries did?
17. What was Njord the god of?
18. What did Vikings do when someone died?
19. What did King Cnut try, and fail to do?
20. What did Vikings believe it was a disgrace to run away from?

19. To command the sea   20. A fight
17. The sea   18. Put their body on board a ship and set fire to it
16. Carried warriors to live in the hall of the brave dead
12. Odin   13. Ragnorak   14. An eight-legged horse   15. Steam
9. Onions   10. Freyja   11. He believed they would die in battle
6. When they were married   7. Glass beads   8. Two ravens
4. Hollowed out cattle horns   5. Soot
1. Runes   2. Strips of woven braid   3. An open-air assembly

Answers:

A metal centre panel on the shield helped to protect the warrior's hand.

Viking women wore their hair long until they were married. They then tied it in a knot at the back of their neck.

When Vikings died, their bodies were placed on a ship that was set on fire so that their souls would sail away to the next world.

The Viking god Thor was said to have pretended to marry a giant who had stolen his magic hammer – Thor wanted to steal it back again!

Other sticker books

You can now have even more fun and collect
all the sticker books in this series

978-1-84236-660-8

978-1-84236-661-5

978-1-84236-303-4

978-1-84236-244-0

978-1-84236-513-7

978-1-84236-304-1

978-1-84236-305-8

978-1-84236-662-2

978-1-84236-302-7

978-1-84236-663-9

978-1-84236-514-4

978-1-84236-255-6

978-1-84236-671-4

978-1-84236-246-4

978-1-84236-307-2

978-1-84236-245-7

978-1-84236-306-5

978-1-84236-669-1

978-1-84236-254-9

978-1-84236-512-0

978-1-84236-247-1

978-1-84236-515-1

978-1-84236-668-4

978-1-84236-672-1

978-1-84236-498-7

TABLE OF CONTENTS

The author wishes to thank *Commentary* and *Judaism* and all other publishers and owners of copyright material for permission granted to use excerpts in the following pages. If any acknowledgment has inadvertently been omitted, apologies are offered.

Part One

THE ESSENCE OF PRESENT-DAY JUDAISM

CHAPTER 1

INTRODUCTION

In the twenty years that have elapsed since the first edition was published, a number of new developments have taken place among the Jewish people, both in and out of Israel. The second part of chapter 1 summarizes some of these changes. A portion of chapter 9 has been replaced with updated material. Chapter 11 is a new addition to this edition.

In 1944, *Commentary's* forerunner, the *Contemporary Jewish Record,* published a symposium containing replies to a set of questions. The symposium aimed to elicit the attitude to Jewishness and the Jewish community on the part of young American Jews representing American literary intelligentsia of Jewish extraction. In the opinion of Norman Podhoretz, *Commentary's* editor, the replies constituted a severe indictment of Judaism and the Jewish community. One of the contributors said that whatever Jewish heritage may have been in the past, in America it has deteriorated into nothingness. Another declared that modern Judaism has produced not a single voice with a note of authority either in philosophy, poetry, rhetorics, let alone in religion. "Who is the American Jew?" asked one of the symposiasts. "What is Jewish in him? What does he believe, especially in these terrible years, that separates him at all from our national habits of acquisitiveness, showiness, and ignorant brag?"

Many things have happened in the world since 1944. The main European Jewish centers were wiped out. The

7

State of Israel emerged. American Jewry moved up to the forefront in the affairs of world Jewry. The vicious anti-Semitism of the 30s declined sharply. Synagogue attendance improved. A resurgent interest in Judaism is in process. The editors of *Commentary* wished to know how these breathtaking world events affected the attitude to Jewishness on the part of young Jewish intellectuals in America today. With this in mind, some fifty questionnaires were sent out. Thirty-one replies were returned, all of which were printed in the April, 1961 issue of *Commentary*. A few months later, the Fall, 1961 issue of *Judaism* published a similar symposium entitled, "My Jewish Affirmation—A Symposium." While the questions posed in the *Judaism* symposium differed in certain respects from those in the *Commentary* symposium, the aim was practically the same.

The two symposia brought together a random group of the most gifted and most articulate young American intellectuals of Jewish birth. They represent diverse geographical, social, and religious backgrounds. Their occupations include representatives of science, arts, and medicine, film producers, publishers, writers, and editors.

Insofar as the contributors in both symposia reflect the present religious state of the Jewish people in America, the picture they portray is practically the same. By and large, however, the *Judaism* group takes a more positive attitude to Jewishness, and several of them display deep insights into the nature of Israel's Covenant faith.

In analyzing the results of *Commentary's* symposium, the editor asks, in what way do today's third- and fourth-generation Jewish intellectuals in America differ in relation to Jewishness from the 1944 group? His answer is: "Hardly at all," except for the fact that they are much less bitter and except for their sympathetic interest in the State of Israel.

However, what is most reassuring—according to *Commentary's* editor—in the attitude of the present generation of young Jewish intellectuals in America is "the atmosphere of idealism that permeates this symposium, an idealism that many of the contributors themselves associate with the fact of their Jewishness. Believing . . . that the essence of Judaism is the struggle for universal justice and human brotherhood, these young intellectuals assert over and over again that anyone who fights for the Ideal is to that degree more Jewish than a man who merely observes the rituals or merely identifies himself with the Jewish community."

That idealism is frequently a dominant trait in the Jewish character is something of which those who know Jewish history are well aware. The questions, however, which need to be answered are: First, since the fight for universal justice and human brotherhood is not confined to Judaism at this juncture of history, what is really the purpose of a distinct Jewish existence? Second, how can these ideals of universal justice and human brotherhood be achieved? How can we reshape this world so that there will be in it no room for men like Hitler, Stalin, and others like them? Can these ideals be realized by secular education, by the promulgation of certain laws, or by the use of police force or military power? Need we perhaps add that recent history has abundantly demonstrated that all these means have failed?

And so it is that the present state of the world makes the Bible—that divine book of history—so terribly relevant for our times. As far back as two thousand years or even three thousand years ago, the Bible taught that universal justice and human brotherhood will come when God will be made supreme in the hearts and affairs of men and nations. To declare this message to the nations was the divine purpose in the creation of Israel. Apart from this mission, Israel's distinct existence has no meaning. And in the light of this mission Jewish history, past and present, can be best understood.

These are some of the weighty matters which prompted this writer to undertake this study. The contributions of both symposia were utilized as the basis for this study. In Part One, a number of excerpts from both symposia were presented which deal with a certain aspect of Judaism and Jewish destiny. The titles appended over each individual contribution reflect—according to this writer—the leading idea of the quoted statement.[1]

Has the religious situation of the Jewish people changed significantly in the twenty years since the printing of the first edition of this study? The answer to this question may be derived from a careful perusal of the material assembled in the *American Jewish Year Book, 1983* (published by the American Jewish Committee and the Jewish Publication Society of America). The following are certain facts and figures pertaining to the religious condition of the American and Israeli Jewish communities.

THE AMERICAN JEWISH COMMUNITY
1. Religious Persuasion

Only 6 percent of American Jews identify themselves as Orthodox, while 62 percent describe themselves as Conservative or Reform Jews; 32 percent are considered secular Jews. 51 percent are affiliated with a synagogue.

2. Religious Practices

22 percent light Sabbath candles regularly. 15 percent observe the dietary laws (two different sets of dishes for meat and

[1]The statements quoted in this Introduction are from the introductory remarks by the Editor of *Commentary* in the April 1961 issue.

dairy products). 5 percent abstain from shopping and working on the Sabbath.

3. Education of Jewish Children

Asked what "predominant form of Jewish education their children had received, are receiving or will receive," the respondents gave the following replies: 12 percent—none; 9 percent—bar/bat mitzvah instruction; 18 percent—Sunday School instruction; 40 percent—Hebrew School education; 7 percent—Yeshiva (Talmudic School), Day School education. The study revealed a decline in Hebrew School attendance.

4. Regular Attendance at Weekly Sabbath Services

Information on regular attendance at the weekly Sabbath services may be obtained from an article in the 1983 *Year Book* entitled "The National Gallup Polls and American Jewish Demography." These Gallup Polls, the findings of which the writer of the article accepts as fairly accurate, and which were conducted during a nine-year period from 1970 through 1979, indicate that 20 percent of Jews affiliated with a synagogue regularly attend the weekly Sabbath services. The correctness of this figure may be attested indirectly by the fact that 22 percent light Sabbath candles regularly. Jews whose homes light Sabbath candles regularly are bound to attend Sabbath services regularly, and Jews who regularly attend Sabbath services are likely to light Sabbath candles regularly.

THE ISRAELI JEWISH COMMUNITY

The Jews in Israel constitute the second-largest Jewish community in the world. In accordance with the findings of the

1983 *Year Book,* some 45 percent of Israeli Jews consider themselves as non-religious or secular Jews. Slightly more than half of the respondents identified themselves as religious Jews, but only 24.2 percent regularly attend the weekly Sabbath services (*Year Book,* p. 7). Jews born in Israel are less religious, and exposure to Israeli society lowers the level of religiosity (p. 22).

Among the conclusions arrived at from this study are the following: Israeli Jews who faithfully observe the rituals of Judaism, such as regular attendance at Sabbath services and abstaining from work on the Sabbath, define themselves as religious; but Israeli Jews who describe themselves as religious do not necessarily adhere to the religious rituals, as proven from the fact that the majority of Israeli Jews travel on the Sabbath (p. 32).

The process of modernization of Israeli society is leading to a lowering of the level of religiosity and an increase in secularization. This does not imply an abandonment of Jewish identification, but rather a development of different forms of religious expression more in harmony with the experiences, temper, and needs of Israeli life (p. 32).

Israeli Jews are becoming polarized into two opposing camps—religious and secular—and there are definite signs that the gap separating the two segments of Israeli Jewry is widening (pp. 31, 33).

CHAPTER 2

HAS JUDAISM BECOME A RELIGION
WITHOUT GOD?

JEWISH TRADITION–A SET OF ETHICAL PRINCIPLES–IN
JUDAISM "KNOWLEDGE AND ACTION ARE PARAMOUNT OVER
FAITH"–INTELLECT AND COMPASSION ARE AT THE CORE OF
THE JEWISH HERITAGE–DO RIGHT–HERE AND NOW–THE
SIGNIFICANT ASPECT OF THE JEWISH TRADITION: ITS
CONCERN WITH THE CONDITION OF MAN–"I HAVE NO
QUARREL WTH RELIGION FOR OTHERS . . ."–THE SUPER-
NATURAL ORIENTATION OF ORTHODOX JUDAISM DESTROYS
ITS EFFECTIVENESS–AMERICAN JEWS ARE EMBRACING THE
SECULAR HUMANITARIAN FAITH OF MANY AMERICAN
GENTILES–"I DO NOT REGARD JEWISHNESS AS PRIMARILY
A MATTER OF RELIGIOUS BELIEF"–OF THE OLD TRIAD OF
JEWISH TRADITION–GOD, TORAH, AND ISRAEL–ISRAEL IS
TODAY THE MOST SIGNIFICANT ASPECT–"JEWISH FAITH IS
A LICENSE FOR SKEPTICISM . . ."–THE RELEVANCE OF
JUDAISM COMES NOT FROM THEOLOGY, DOGMAS, OR CREED
–JEWISH RELIGIOUS PRACTICE DEMANDS LITTLE FAITH–
PRESENT-DAY JUDAISM: A TRADITION WTHOUT GOD–THE
SECULARIZATION OF AMERICAN JUDAISM

I. JEWISH TRADITION—A SET OF ETHICAL PRINCIPLES

"FOR ME THE [JEWISH] TRADITION represents a set of generally congenial ethical principles; an attachment to a history of suffering by kinsmen; valuable character traits (learned, not inherited) and intellectual virtues; and a religion that asks and answers its ultimate questions in a positively sane manner. . . . I do not practice any religion."[1]

II. IN JUDAISM "KNOWLEDGE AND ACTION ARE PARAMOUNT OVER FAITH"

"I am firmly rooted in the Jewish tradition; having grown up happily in a richly Jewish home. I believe that in four key respects Judaism is unsurpassed in Western religion. (A) It has consistently applied its ethical insights, for which its spokesmen showed a remarkable talent very early in history, to a variety of mundane matters, at the same time keeping its sights on distant goals such as universal peace. (B) It is explicitly tolerant of other points of view. (C) It makes minimum demands on credulity, and concentrates on the human, physical, and practical. Knowledge and action are paramount over faith. It is refreshingly free from cloying otherworldliness, emetic concern for the 'soul,' and biological nonsense. (D) It has led, in its adherents, to a frequent and attractive combination of attitudes: idealism and skepticism . . .

"I believe that most Americans can lead a fruitful, decent, and happy life in any of the popular religious traditions. I have the uneasy feeling that in most cases religious conversion in America in any direction reflects more on the

[1]Aaron Asher, in *Commentary* (New York), April, 1961.

emotional instability of the person involved than on the merits of the religions."[2]

III. INTELLECT AND COMPASSION ARE AT THE CORE OF THE JEWISH HERITAGE

"My life has had little that is specifically Jewish about it in the usual sense. I never had any religious training, I was never Bar Mitzvah'd, I never learned to speak or read Hebrew, and I have visited far more churches and cathedrals than synagogues. I don't say this in a belligerent tone, but simply as a statement of fact; I haven't consciously rejected conventional Judaism, but simply drifted away from it.

"Yet I wonder if there isn't some flavor of Jewishness left, even after Kashrut and T'fillin and Yom Kippur[3] have been discarded. As a college professor and a critic of American foreign policy, I think I detect in myself some measure of those twin qualities of intellect and compassion that were always at the heart of the Jewish heritage, and that can endure after the abandonment of formal religious practices. I apply myself now to the study of U.S. relations with Latin America, a subject far removed from the traditional areas of Hebrew learning. But something Jewish somehow survives, something that I would not willingly let die. I think that Jewish culture, taken in the broadest sense, has an enormous influence not only upon American life, but upon the life of all mankind. It seems to me only a small, and in a Jew pardonable, exaggeration to say that the world in which we live is dominated by the ideas of a handful of Jews—Karl Marx, Sigmund Freud, and Albert

[2]Enoch Gordis, in *Commentary* (New York), April, 1961.
[3]Kashrut—observance of the dietary laws; T'fillin—the use of phylacteries at the morning prayer; Yom Kippur—observance of the Day of Atonement.

Einstein (to say nothing of Jesus and St. Paul). These men also rejected much or all of traditional Judaism, but I see in them those same qualities of compassion and intellect that I discover, on a vastly reduced scale, in myself."[4]

IV. DO RIGHT—HERE AND NOW

"From *Commentary's* recent symposium and the spate of laudatory and critical correspondence that followed, it would seem that contemporary views of Judaism constitute a wide continuum along whose range all of us who call ourselves Jews can find some place. This may not be very satisfying, but I prefer it to the alternative of having someone step forward and issue his ukase as to just what Judaism is, while the rest of us Jews settle down as heretics outside the fold . . .

"The Jews were always on the outside looking inside, sort of wanting to be inside, but at the same time savoring that position of being outside with a stubbornness and even pride in being different and in not giving in. But it was not simply a stubborn refusal to give in. There is [in the Jew] the element of this-worldliness, the conviction that it is this side of the abyss that must be made to operate properly, with the concentration on the acts, on the behavior, on the interrelation of man with man in his specific transactions, and not simply on his Sunday morning behavior or his belated repentance. Do right or try to do right here and now, not tomorrow or in the next world . . . Who is to say that this is not the essence of Judaism?

"In the end, however, the affirmation of any single Jew is a social and cultural problem with a complexity that will hardly bear analysis and with aspects that may be superficial or profound but all of them important . . . My own

[4]Samuel Shapiro, in *Commentary* (New York), April, 1961.

conviction is that it[5] is more than lighting candles on Friday night and fasting on Yom Kippur and it may not even include these."[6]

V. THE SIGNIFICANT ASPECT OF THE JEWISH TRADITION: ITS CONCERN WITH THE PRESENT CONDITION OF MAN

"The essentials of Judaism were never clearly presented to me in terms which I could understand as a student and I could scarcely affirm that I understand the faith into which I was born." In order to be able to answer the questions in the symposium this participant consulted a number of books, and he came across the following passage in *The Standard Jewish Encyclopedia* which appealed to him, as it expressed his views on the subject under consideration.

> Moreover, Judaism places the emphasis on practical religion rather than on dogma. The prophets of Israel insisted that only he who showed justice, love and mercy really "knew" God, and the Pentateuch demands "the doing of all the words of this Law" rather than the probing of "secret things which are the Lord's." Right action rather than contemplation has been the central theme of Judaism, notwithstanding the fact that contemplation does play a great part in its mystical tradition.—Cecil Roth (ed.), *The Standard Jewish Encyclopedia* (New York: 1959), pp. 1078-1079.

"To a social scientist serving as a professor of social welfare in a graduate school in a university, these words held a considerable meaning.

"To me one aspect of the Jewish tradition which I re-

[5]i.e., the meaning of Judaism and Jewishness.
[6]Nathan A. Greenberg, in *Judaism* (New York), Fall, 1961.

gard as centrally significant is the concern of Judaism with the condition of man as well as his concern with God . . . In my teaching, study and research I am primarily concerned with the condition of man on this earth. I have little interest in 'the hereafter' . . . The most important consequence of this central aspect of the Jewish tradition is a doctrine of social responsibility which I regard as absolutely essential to human life and survival."[7]

VI. "I HAVE NO QUARREL WITH RELIGION FOR OTHERS . . ."

"I believe my Jewish affirmation is similar to that of many other third-generation American Jewish intellectuals. I am not religious, and I don't think it so terribly important that I bear the physical mark of a Son of the Covenant. Further, many Jewish customs—both religious and secular—strike me as do other folk customs of, say, the Irish or Italians: They seem to be quaint and primitive, and characteristic of a village society rather than of a metropolitan society . . . So much for the negative side.

"There are two major reasons for my positive Jewish affirmation. In the first place, I recognize certain Jewish cultural values as among the worthiest mankind has ever produced. These include stress on learning and rationalism, the emphasis on justice and law, the deeply ingrained acceptance of respect for man and individual deviation . . .

"My second major source of Jewish affirmation arises out of my identification with the underdog. Both as an American and as a Jew, I believe in the equality of man (not biologically or culturally, of course, but under God and the law). When prejudice and selfish interests deprive any individual or group of equal rights, I rebel. I am

[7]Albert Rose, in *Judaism* (New York), Fall, 1961.

proud to be a Jew if only because Jews have been a persecuted people and have fought against the persecution of
other peoples . . . I have no quarrel with religion for
others: I believe I have a strong sense of ethics and social
responsibility without it."[8]

VII. THE SUPERNATURAL ORIENTATION OF ORTHODOX JUDAISM DESTROYS ITS EFFECTIVENESS

"On looking back, I can see at least four major experiences in my adult life which took me from reluctant Judaism to proud affirmation—both in feeling and action.
These are: 1. Psychoanalysis, 2. Israel, 3. Parenthood, and
4. Reconstructionism . . .

"Psychoanalysis has deepened my understanding of
others as well as myself . . . Working closely with a non-
Jew whose integrity and honesty I trusted, I was helped to
see that many feelings I had toward people who were not
Jewish were unreasonable projections of my own. As I
became aware of my own prejudicial judgments of Gentiles, I was less dismayed by anti-Semitism and better
equipped to deal with it . . .

"Ever since the destruction of the Temple in 70 C.E.
Jews have seen themselves as a sinning, guilt-ridden people
who had fallen out of Divine Grace. Israel[9] put an end to
this nonsense . . .

"Parenthood is not a one-way street. I have learned a
good deal from the sweet clarity of a child's view of the
world. For example I quote the wisdom of my four-year-
old son's definition of God. One morning at breakfast
after intently listening to a discussion about God, he softly

[8]Arnold M. Rose, in *Judaism* (New York), Fall, 1961.
[9]The State of Israel.

volunteered, 'I know what God is.' Naturally we stopped to listen. 'God,' he continued, 'is that part of your life that you don't know much about.'

Reconstructionism with its "concept of Judaism as a civilization has greatly helped me organize and formulate my vague ideas. Judaism, as represented by the Orthodox tradition, seems to be fixed on the dead past, not the living past. The worship of God takes the form of a plea for forgiveness . . . Furthermore, its supernatural orientation and belief in revelation destroys its effectiveness for me as a meaningful tradition. Conservatism and Reform Judaism while superficially more permissive do not provide any rationale for this permissiveness. They are just as willing to hold onto meaningless practice even though English is substituted for Hebrew."[10]

VIII. AMERICAN JEWS ARE EMBRACING THE SECULAR HUMANITARIAN FAITH OF MANY AMERICAN GENTILES

"I think that the situation of the American Jew has changed radically since World War II and that the change has most affected my generation, the generation that fought the war and is now in the neighborhood of forty . . . The change I have in mind is the opening to Jews of so many vocations, and consequently of so many social milieus, that were once considered closed to them . . . The effect on their Jewishness is to make them think less about it . . . Judaism, as a thing to be accepted or rejected, is less of an issue in our lives. For it looks less like the position of an embattled minority . . . and more . . . like one of those liberal Protestant denominations to which so many Americans loosely belong.

[10]Marvin I. Shapiro, in *Judaism* (New York), Fall, 1961.

"It can be said that American Jews are simply assimilating as the Jews did in Western Europe fifty years ago, but there is, I think, a difference in that Jews here are following a general American movement peculiar to our time. You have only to teach the older literature to realize how few students seem to know any more what, according to their religious affiliations, they are supposed to believe, that all in fact subscribe to the same secular, democratic, humanitarian faith—belief in a more or less impersonal deity and in tolerance, good will, peace, progress, and social justice. The truth is that American Jews are not so much going Protestant as that all Americans, including Protestants, are shedding divisive traditional identities in favor of a new American amalgam."[11]

IX. "I DO NOT REGARD JEWISHNESS AS PRIMARILY A MATTER OF RELIGIOUS BELIEF"

". . . I have tried to make it clear that I do not regard Jewishness as primarily a matter of religious belief. The most profound and valuable insight of Judaic religion was, I believe, the ideal of universal justice, and this has become so permanent a part of Western civilization that it is no longer distinctively either a Jewish or a religious ideal."[12]

X. OF THE OLD TRIAD OF JEWISH TRADITION— GOD, TORAH, AND ISRAEL—ISRAEL IS TODAY THE MOST SIGNIFICANT ASPECT

"My personal relationship to Judaism (defined as the thoughts and practices of Jewish civilization) provides the basis for my ties to the American Jewish community, the State of Israel, and the Jewish People. I consider the tie

[11]Robert Langbaum, in *Commentary* (New York), April, 1961.
[12]Raziel Abelson, in *Commentary* (New York), April, 1961.

of Jewish peoplehood to be the fundamental tie that binds Jews the world over and which forms the basis for creative Jewish survival in our age . . . I consider the events of the past seventy or eighty years in Jewish history as part of, or contributing to, the Zionist revolution which has been the most profound event in Jewish life since the development of the Oral Law[13] . . . The disruption of the common belief in the traditional triad[14] came, for the bulk of our people, less than a century ago. It was in order to salvage the tradition and use it to devise new patterns for the creative survival of the Jewish People, that the Zionists implicitly turned to the concept of Israel—as land and as people . . . Though I would personally not speak of the lessened importance of God and Torah, as aspects of the well-known triad, it seems that our age requires Israel (peoplehood) to serve as the most significant aspect of Jewish tradition."[15]

XI. "JEWISH FAITH IS A LICENSE FOR SKEPTICISM . . ."

"Jewish faith is a license for skepticism: our calling is to destroy idols . . . In world intellectual history, insofar as Jewish thought is distinctive, it is distinguished by its nonconformity. In its own tradition, there is resistance even to togetherness with God: Abraham presumed to give Him advice, and Job to bring Him to justice. I applaud this frame of mind . . . Social ethics, an independent spirit, esteem for the mind, and an integrated self—these are the things I find significant and viable in the Jewish tradition . . .

"The current Jewish revival in America seems to me

[13]The Talmud.
[14]"God, Torah and Israel are one."
[15]Daniel J. Elazar, in *Judaism* (New York), Fall, 1961.

more marked by a change in status than by a growth in substance. It is a return but not yet a revitalization . . . Isaiah might proclaim again, 'What to Me are your burnt offerings!' for ritual has gained new acceptance but not always on the basis of renewed contents."[16]

XII. THE RELEVANCE OF JUDAISM COMES NOT FROM THEOLOGY, DOGMAS, OR CREED

"What is especially significant about the Jewish tradition is its relevance for our own age with its problems and perplexities. This relevance does not derive from a system of theology, or a set of dogmas, or a closed creed, but from a series of insights into the nature of man and the structure of the world. These insights developed gradually, and often in anguish and crisis, among the Jewish people and its prophets and teachers out of their collective experience, and was extolled by many as Heilsgeschichte."[17]

XIII. JEWISH RELIGIOUS PRACTICE DEMANDS LITTLE FAITH

"A part of the Jewish tradition which speaks strongly to me is suggested in a phrase from the New Year's services, the 'bond of life.' I know this refers primarily to the relation between the dead and the living, but it also seems to echo significantly throughout the whole of Jewish life and thought. There are suggestions of the messianic hope, the mystery of Jewish survival, the fortitude of the suffering servant, the respect for learning and spirituality, the impulse to ethical transcendence, a commitment to justice, a devotion to life itself. The bond of life demands that we

[16]Abraham Kaplan, in *Judaism* (New York), Fall, 1961.
[17]i.e., redemptive history. Israel Knox, in *Judaism* (New York), Fall, 1961.

love more when we perceive a lack of love in the world, that we be more in the world than of it . . .

"What interests and puzzles me, however, is the number of aspects of the Jewish tradition which seem so much at variance with this impulse . . . How could the idea of the hallowing of life turn into legalism and rigidity? . . .

"Jewish self-consciousness is surely connected with the tradition's relative lack of employment for the individual soul and conscience. Except for monotheism, the question is rarely raised what must one believe to be a Jew, because Jewish identity has usually been a matter of belonging rather than belief . . . I went to Reform Sunday Schools and did not grow up in a religious household or one particularly imbued with Jewish culture . . . And, although I was confirmed by Milton Steinberg, I was at that time quite antagonistic to religious thought generally, so if his example affected me it was not in any direct sense. I'm puzzled and sobered to realize how little the demand of belief is made upon me in so much of Jewish ceremony and worship."[18]

XIV. PRESENT-DAY JUDAISM: A TRADITION WITHOUT GOD

"I have a memory of a noble religion in which I no longer believe, nor was taught to believe, and of a heroic struggle in which I have never participated . . .

"*Commentary* has skipped over a vital point. It has concerned itself with the upholding of Jewish traditions and the Jewish community and has totally ignored the question of fidelity to a Jewish God. The great thing about the Jews is precisely their religion. This is their magnificent contribution to the world, this is what preserved them and

[18]Sonya Rudikoff, in *Commentary* (New York), April, 1961.

this is what killed them. They died for their God—and not for some bastardized 'culture' . . . The use of a temple as a social institution, the deifying and romanticizing of an abstract Jewish culture is a vulgarization . . . and sinful and impudent in the face of what Jews have really died for.

"When one gives up a belief in God, one ought to have the strength to give up the forms associated with religious observance . . . Jews should realize the enormity of their giving up of religion, and to be aware at least of when they have actually done this. As a culture in limbo in America, which is a country which breaks up all traditions, they are doomed to eventual extinction and all the trumped-up Chanukahs[19] in the world won't make a particle of difference."[20]

XV. THE SECULARIZATION OF AMERICAN JUDAISM

The utterances cited above represent the voice of the Jewish laity. It is, therefore, fitting, to conclude the series with a statement from a rabbinical spokesman. The following is a summary containing a number of the high points from an article in a later issue in *Judaism* in which the writer presents a keen analysis of the religious state of the American Jewish community.

A survey of present-day Jewish literature—we are told—reveals a concentration on subjects of anti-Semitism, Jewish education, Jewish contributions, Judaism and democracy, the Jewish family, the synagogue, the problem of Jewish

---

[19]Chanukah—Feast of Dedication or Feast of Lights—to commemorate the victory of the Maccabees against the de-Judaizing policies of Antiochus IV; this feast often falls at the same time as Christmas, and in certain Jewish circles is used to counteract any possible effect which the meaning of Christmas may exert upon the Jews.
[20]Barbara Probst Solomon, in *Commentary* (New York), April, 1961.

religious observances, etc., etc. But there is a strange absence in these discussions of the forthrightly religious and God-oriented concepts of ancient Jewish tradition.

There is a tendency in American Judaism to glorify the human element, as seen from its one-sided approach to certain Biblical teachings about human nature. Stress is laid on man's exalted position as the crown of Creation, in accordance with such Biblical passages as, "And God created man in his own image" (Genesis 1:27), and "Thou hast made him [i.e., man] a little lower than the angels" (Psalm 8:5 [8:6 Heb.]). Little consideration is given to the fact that the same Bible also teaches that man has an inborn disposition to evil, as in the passage, "For the inclination of man's heart is evil from his very youth" (Genesis 8:21).

American Judaism ignores the somber lessons of human failure implicit in Biblical history, as, for example, when the record of creation is followed almost immediately by the account of fratricidal murder by Adam's firstborn son. Of like significance is the tendency to gloss over the Biblical reports of Israel's repeated failures before God, as when the rejoicing occasioned by the deliverance from the Egyptian bondage and the miraculous crossing of the Red Sea quickly gave way to a mood of rebellion at the first encounter of a temporary water shortage; or when the spirit of godly fear and self-surrender manifested by the people at the Sinai revelation soon evaporated in the intoxicating orgy of the golden calf incident.

Messianism, which in the Bible is described as God's mighty interposition in human history, has become debased by contemporary Jewish spokesmen into something of a socio-economic program to be achieved by man alone by way of progressive, evolutionary fulfillment. The prophetic teachings concerning the day of judgment in which God will put an end to history as we know it are completely disregarded.

While in the Bible enforced exile is equivalent to alienation from God, in contemporary Jewish religious thinking the concept of exile has been divested of its religious connotation and distorted into a socio-political state of physical uprootedness.

In Biblical and post-Biblical Jewish theology man is represented as having both a good and an evil inclination. Evil passions are a basic ingredient of human nature. Human life is, therefore, marked by spiritual tension. But with God's help man can attain victory over his evil impulse, and man's spiritual conflicts may even become the means of strengthening his moral fiber and ennobling his spiritual stature. All this, of course, is rooted in the belief that God is both just and merciful, which means that He destroys the unrepentant evildoer and is full of compassion toward those of a contrite heart.

But this ancient Jewish theology runs counter to the shallow spirituality of American Judaism. The result is that not even the intense spiritual atmosphere of the High Holiday season can shake the American Jew out of his spiritual lethargy. It explains the lack of real personal involvement of the present-day Jewish worshipers at the High Holiday services. The various proposals suggested to remedy this situation, such as the introduction of more ritual and symbolism, more congregational singing, study or discussion, or shortening of the time of the services, have all proven ineffective. This failure is due to the fact that the proposed measures are external and technical, while the malady is religious in substance. The essence of the High Holiday theme is human sin, individual and collective, and the need for self-examination and repentance. Without a belief in a personal God to whom man is held accountable, without the acknowledgment of the reality and relevance of sin in human life and the need for divine forgiveness, there can be no real change in the attitude of the Jew to his religion. American Jews are in desperate need of gaining religious conviction.[21]

[21]Rabbi Norman E. Frimer, "The A-Theological Judaism Of The American Community," *Judaism*, Spring, 1962. (At the time of the writing of this article, Dr. Frimer was Director of the B'nai Brith Hillel Foundation at Brooklyn College.)

CHAPTER 3

OPPOSITION TO CHRISTIANITY

"I SEE NO VIRTUES UNIQUE to the Jewish tradition, and some evils. The main evil—and here I follow Nietzsche—is that the Jews invented Christianity. And the Jewish tradition ultimately bears some responsibility for Nazism, for the latter is Old Testament racism stood on its head. The claim that the Jews (or any other racial or religious group) are in any sense 'chosen people' is a total lie, with disastrous consequences of world-historical dimensions for Jew and non-Jew alike."[1]

The author of the above statement, one of the participants in the symposia, represents himself as an atheist who hopes that any children he has will become atheists. His is the atheist variety of anti-Christianity which often wears an anti-Semitic garb.[2] He also expresses the anti-Christian attitude of communism. It is remarkable how often the name of Karl Marx appears in the symposia. Some of the participants seem to consider him as a worthy representative of the Jewish tradition, or they feel that his place in history gives credit to the Jewish people. Actually, this writer knows of no anti-Semite who used more hateful language when speaking of Jews than Karl Marx did.[3] Russia, which is the headquarters of world Marxism, is

[1]Ned Polsky, in *Commentary* (New York), April, 1961.
[2]Will Herberg, *Judaism and Modern Man* (New York: Farrar, Strauss & Young, Inc., 1951), pp. 273-4; Maurice Samuel, *The Great Hatred* (New York: Alfred A. Knopf, Inc., 1940), pp. 127-8.
[3]Karl Marx, *A World Without Jews*, translated from original German by Dagobert J. Runes (New York 16: Philosophical Library, 1959).

today probably the most anti-Semitic country in the world.

The Jewish variety of anti-Christianity was expressed by another participant in the symposia as seen in the passage below:

"There does not seem to me a complex of values or aspirations or beliefs that continue to connect one Jew to another in our country, but rather an ancient and powerful disbelief, which, if it is not fashionable or wise to assert in public, is no less powerful for being underground: that is, the rejection of the myth of Jesus as Christ. Not only does this serve to separate the Jew from his Christian neighbor on the one side who accepts Jesus, but also from the man on his other side who is indifferent, and even from the fellow across the street, the downright atheist, whose tradition, whose social history and bias, do not lead him to reject the Christian saviour with quite the same quality of willfulness, zeal, and blood certainty.

"And wherein my fellow Jews reject Jesus as the supernatural envoy of God, I feel a kinship with them. It is not the sort of kinship, however, that produces solidarity and trust between us—for the strength with which Jesus continues to be rejected is not equalled by the passion with which the God who gave the Law to Moses is embraced, or approached . . . The result is that we are bound together, I to my fellow Jews, my fellow Jews to me, in a relationship that is peculiarly enervating and unviable. Our rejection, our abhorrence finally, of the Christian phantasy leads us to proclaim to the world that we are Jews still—alone, however, what have we to proclaim to one another?"[4]

To the informed American Christian who is a genuine follower of Jesus Christ, the above lines may make painful reading because of the following considerations: The Prot-

[4]Philip Roth, in *Commentary* (New York), April, 1961.

estant Reformation, which has been a movement back to Biblical Christianity, has gradually brought about a decided improvement in the status of the Jew in the countries under the influence of the revived Biblical faith. The beginning of America has its roots in Protestant Christianity. True Biblical Christianity is probably stronger in America than in any part of Christendom. America has for a long time been a haven of refuge for oppressed Jews. It is not possible to dissociate America's kind treatment of the Jewish people from the Christian faith of this country.

Nor is the State of Israel without bearing on this question. Those who know the history of Zionism are aware of the sympathetic interest which evangelical Christianity displayed in the Zionist movement. And today Israel's greatest enemies belong to countries under communism and Islam, while most of its friends are found in the lands of Christendom.

To return to the above anti-Christian statement. The only unusual feature about it is, perhaps, its excessive frankness. There has been in certain Jewish quarters a steady effort to sing the praises of Judaism and at the same time to downgrade the Christian faith. Christianity is described as a pessimistic, sin-and-guilt-obsessed religion, abstracted from the realities of everyday life, dwelling too much on the hereafter. "Whereas Christianity," we are told, "emphasizes flight from the world, Judaism stresses the employment of God's blessings in the world."[5]

It is high time to set the record straight. From its very inception, Christianity has been the faith of the most cultured and civilized part of the world, and for centuries Christendom has been in the forefront in science, medicine, industry, commerce, art, and culture. In the last

[5]Ernst Jacob, *Universal Jewish Encyclopedia* (New York: The Universal Jewish Encyclopedia, Inc., 1939), III, p. 186.

hundred years thousands of the finest and most educated young men and women have left the comforts of civilization and gone out to faraway places in Asia and Africa. There they have taught the natives modern methods of agriculture and industry, founded schools and universities, opened hospitals, established leprosaria for the treatment of leprosy and often contracted the disease in the process of taking care of others. They taught the natives to read and write, and since in many of those parts the natives had no written language of their own, these representatives of Jesus Christ often had to create written languages. As a matter of fact, these Christian activities often instilled in the natives a desire for a better way of life and indirectly prepared them for the assumption of political independence.

This writer is personally acquainted with the following lay Christian movements in this country: The Christian Medical Society, the American Scientific Affiliation, the Christian Businessmen's Committee, the International Christian Leadership and the Faith-at-Work movement. Affiliated with these groups are men and women occupying the highest positions in science, industry, medicine, government, and business. These are men and women who are dedicated to God and the ideals of Christianity. They come together for Bible reading and prayer and seek to apply their Christian faith in their personal, family, and social life. Many of the largest and best universities and colleges in America have been established by dedicated Christians and church bodies. The same is true of many of our hospitals. Then there are many organizations, like the Salvation Army and Alcoholics Anonymous, which day in and day out are engaged in the task of rehabilitating broken human lives. Surely a world religion so much progressive, so much aggressive, and so much committed to the task of making this world a better place to live can hardly be called a flight-from-the-world religion.

On the other hand, those who have first-hand knowledge of traditional Judaism, the kind of Judaism which for centuries dominated the whole of Jewish life, realize that this Judaism was indeed a flight from the world.

It encouraged Jewish preoccupation with the study of the Talmud—the Rabbinic Torah—even though much of it is of irrelevant nature. It held secular education in low esteem. Its ideal for the Jewish husband was to be able to spend his days in the Beth Hamidrash,[6] poring over talmudic studies, while his wife worked to support the family.

Modern Jewish participation in business, industry, politics, art, and the professions have begun with a revolt against traditional Judaism. The most progressive and prosperous Jewish communities in Europe were those in Western Europe, and consisted of Jews who broke away from traditional Judaism. The Jews of Eastern Europe, which until the Nazi era was the world's stronghold of traditional Judaism, were the least progressive Jews in Christendom. Those Jews in Eastern Europe who in the era between the two world wars were most active economically, in education, and in politics, and the Jews from Eastern Europe who emigrated to America were openly hostile to traditional Judaism.

Palestinian Jewry that lived in Palestine under the Turkish regime represented traditional Judaism, but socially, culturally, and economically it differed little from its Arab neighbors. The Jews who emigrated to Palestine to rebuild the country were predominantly opposed to traditional Judaism. In fact, Zionist leadership consisted

---

[6]House of Study, usually a synagogue.

mostly of nonreligious Jews. The State of Israel is being built up by Jews who use methods and the know-how which they acquired in the countries of Christendom. The Jews who come to Israel from Islamic countries are steeped in traditional Judaism, but are two or three centuries behind in culture as compared with the Jews from Christendom.

"The Jew in America, as in other countries," we are told by one of the participants in the symposia, "has supplied a high degree of skills and creativity to the intellectual and the economic life of the nation . . . Yet for these very qualities the Jews are indebted to the culture from which they have most suffered. One of the greatest periods of Jewish creativity was begun by the Jews who had been emancipated from the life and mentality of the ghetto by the Napoleonic reforms. Not Orthodox Judaism, but Western civilization was the intellectual source of this genius."[7] "In many ways Orthodox Judaism is a mystic flight from reality . . ."[8]

In view of the above facts, how is one to explan the anti-Christian attitude of certain American Jews? How are we to account for the perennial drive to prevent Christian children from singing Christmas carols, the recitation of the Lord's Prayer, and the reading of the Bible in public schools? This writer knows of no more satisfactory answer than the one given by two of the participants in the symposia, as seen from the following excerpts:

> One meets very few actively practicing Catholics in and around a large university; when a Catholic turns against his religion . . . however opposed he may now be to religious articles of faith in general, he can understand

[7]Lionel Rogosin, in *Commentary* (New York), April, 1961.
[8]Selwyn G. Geller, in *Judaism* (New York), Fall, 1961.

how it is that others may retain their faith. Perhaps there are several reasons for this, but at any rate one reason seems to be the fact that he was raised in his religion, and there was no ambiguity of attitude toward it in his home. The striking characteristic about us, on the other hand, is that we find it quite incredible that anyone should actively believe in a body of religious dogma. . . . It fascinates us to think that there are those who believe, and we may even try to provoke such beliefs in ourselves, but in the end we cannot really imagine what it is like. . . . And the only thing to which I can consciously trace this utter inability to understand the feelings of the true believer is the sense I had from my earliest years that belief was not demanded of me, that it was not even expected that I should or supposed that I would. Belief had no role to play. Judaism itself of course calls for very little active belief in dogma. . . .[9]

. . . I also observe the "Jewish" organizations, heavy with money and access to the media of public communication that only money can buy, for whom the Jew's relationship to his God is a topic of very little interest. Instead, they are busy with such projects as the eradication of all manifestations of Christianity from American public life, manifestations to which they object, it can be suspected, not so much because they are Christian as because they are religious and take seriously the Word of God as a genuine event in human history.[10]

[9]Judith Jarvis, in *Commentary* (New York), April, 1961.
[10]Michael Wyschogrod, in *Judaism* (New York), Fall, 1961.

CHAPTER 4

THE STRUGGLE BACK TO GOD

OURS IS AN AGE OF LONGING AND GROPING—HOLINESS OF
THE INDIVIDUAL IS THE ESSENCE OF JUDAISM—THE
BIBLICAL ENCOUNTER BETWEEN MAN AND GOD, THE
BIBLICAL COVENANT, TOTAL COMMITMENT TO GOD—THESE
ARE THE ESSENCE OF JUDAISM—RELIGIOUS FAITH FREELY
CHOSEN, NOT SOCIOLOGICAL BEHAVIOR, IS THE ESSENCE
OF JEWISHNESS—THE ONGOING PROCESS OF SIFTING AND
SEPARATION

I. OURS IS AN AGE OF LONGING AND GROPING

"It is now apparent that the much publicized revival of
religion in this country since the Second World War has
been a revival of formal religious affiliation rather than of
religious faith. Our age is not an age of return; it has more
properly been characterized as an age of longing. Socialism,
scientism, and other secular ideologies have been found
wanting as objects of total allegiance and this has induced
a groping for a new focus of ultimate concern. This groping is especially poignant in Jewish circles because the
phenomenal success of the Zionist movement in helping
to create the State of Israel has robbed Zionism of much
of the fervor that enabled it to serve as a substitute for
religion for so many American Jews . . .

"For all the return to religion in the past fifteen years,
the American Jewish community remains a community of
citizens of Western civilization seeking Jewish roots rather
than a community of Jews seeking a rapport with Western

civilization. The estranged Jew of today does not have a Torah-centered community to provide the rhythms and gratification for which he would then find a rationale . . .

"In past ages, a religious thinker could engage in theology with a profound sense of the difficulties involved but with confidence that answers were to be won. In our age, the theological enterprise itself has become questionable and with it religion . . . It is one thing to say that I cannot believe in the God of the fathers in the way they believed in Him, it is another thing to wonder whether one can believe in Him at all. Faith remains more a struggle than a gift, but for me it is the crucial Jewish struggle, since a Judaism without God strikes me as idolatrous tribalism."[1]

II. HOLINESS OF THE INDIVIDUAL IS THE ESSENCE OF JUDAISM

"Judaism is not a sacerdotal religion. It has no priests who can claim supernatural powers. The priests were Temple functionaries who were maintained because they played a part in Temple rites, but they laid claim to no supernatural powers to bind or loosen, to bless or curse . . .

"Nor do the rabbis (except the wonder-working rebbaiem) claim to have heavenly powers that are denied to the priests. They were not to make up a clerical caste. The rabbis were the scholars and the teachers . . . It is only in modern times that the rabbis tended to become the Jewish clergy, a professional class; and this is a development that is unfortunate both for Judaism and the rabbis themselves . . .

"The ideal of Judaism remains, however, unaltered: 'But ye shall be unto me a kingdom of priests and a holy nation.' This has always been interpreted as meaning that

[1]Malcolm L. Diamond, in *Commentary* (New York), April, 1961.

each individual can become a 'priest,' that is, allow all his actions to be directed by God, so that he may take on himself the kingdom of heaven. As Isaiah put it: 'But ye shall be named the priests of God, men shall call you the ministers of our God.' These words were not spoken to any one class in Israel, but to all Israel, to every man, woman, and child. With all due respect for the great Hillel,[2] were I asked to state the essence of Judaism, I would answer in the words of Leviticus 20:7 '. . . be ye holy: for I am the Lord your God.' "[3]

III. THE BIBLICAL ENCOUNTER BETWEEN MAN AND GOD, THE BIBLICAL COVENANT, TOTAL COMMITMENT TO GOD—THESE ARE THE ESSENCE OF JUDAISM

"By the Biblical dialogue I mean that view implicit through the Hebrew Bible that man realizes his uniqueness and attains true human and personal existence through 'walking humbly' with God . . . It is the really serious confession of the oneness of God by the man who loves God with all his heart, soul, mind and might, the man who gives God the sacrifice of a broken and a contrite heart and who lives his whole life in the face of God.

"The Biblical covenant is that mutual commitment within the dialogue with God that makes Israel a people. It is the covenant to become 'a kingdom of priests and a holy nation'—to take seriously God's kingship by building true community in which every aspect of man's personal and social life is brought into the dialogue with God . . . So far as I can see it is this covenant alone that binds together all the generations of Israel and gives some common

[2]Hillel the Elder. His opinion concerning the essence of Judaism is referred to in Part Two of this study.
[3]Milton R. Konvitz, in *Judaism* (New York), Fall, 1961.

meaning to the name Jew. I cannot understand those variants of modern Judaism that set it aside in favor of universal ideals, reason, or 'religious civilization.' To me the survival of the Jewish people takes on religious meaning and value to the extent that the Jews take on themselves, in each new situation, the task of the covenant. By the same token, intermarriage is not, to me, an evil per se, but only insofar as it hinders this task. The unique task for which Israel is 'chosen' implies no superiority over other peoples and certainly no Jewish exclusiveness such as is manifest in so many modern Jewish communities where Jewish belonging and culture are ends in themselves, divorced from the primary religious commitment to become a holy people.

" 'God asks for the heart,' says Bahya ibn Pequda . . . No amount and variety of Jewish communal activities can make up for the lack of it . . .

"I believe the [Jewish] tradition could be better preserved and enhanced if we gave up once and for all the essentially Greek understanding of Torah as law and went back to the biblical understanding of Torah as God's guidance in dialogue with him . . .

"My Jewish outlook and commitment is, indeed, a fundamental source for my total life orientation. The Psalms, Job, the prophets, the sayings of the Fathers,[4] the Tales of the Hasidim[5] speak to me more deeply than any other literature or tradition. The biblical emuna, the trust that walks with God even through the valley of the shadow of death, stands at the heart of my personal faith and my religious thought."[6]

[4]Refers to the Pirkē Abot in the Mishnah.
[5]Hasidism, a Jewish pietist movement which appeared in the eighteenth century.
[6]Maurice Friedman, in *Judaism* (New York), Fall, 1961.

IV. RELIGIOUS FAITH FREELY CHOSEN, NOT SOCIOLOGICAL BEHAVIOR, IS THE ESSENCE OF JEWISHNESS

". . . the tendency among North American Jews to demonstrate to our Gentile neighbors that we are really no different from them in so far as essentials are concerned, that being a Jew is like rooting for the Yankees rather than the Red Sox (which, after all, is a privilege that North American democracy permits every citizen) is, like the anti-Semitism it seeks to conquer, based on a faulty concept of human nature. (I am therefore skeptical of certain tendencies in North America to settle our anxieties by hiding behind the comfort of a rationalistic humanism for which existence is a night in which all cows are black.)

"I affirm therefore that the essence of Jewishness is religious faith, not sociological behavior . . . Persons are Jews . . . only to the extent to which they accept the Jewish faith. This faith . . . lies in a total commitment to an all-consuming primeval experience in which the Jewish people as a whole was challenged into existence. This existence took the form of a Divine human covenant in which God, by the very act of revealing Himself to us, at the same time bound us to the promise to realize His commandments . . . Thus Israel was born in revelation, and through the historic experience of this revelation, and the attempt to embody its commandments into concrete existence, is continuously reborn.

". . . Professor Fackenheim reminds us that implicit in the covenant is a factor of great importance to every Jew, namely, the Messianic promise. For the Jew, the anticipation of the Messiah—according to which we act and hope—

is a point at which both the past and the present can acquire ultimate meaning. Indeed one might argue that this very anticipation is part of the promised redemption. To exist as a Jew, therefore, is to experience oneself as being between Revelation, on the one hand, and Redemption, on the other."

When Jewish existence is "founded on a commitment derived from revelation," it is inevitably attended by a kind of alienation which this participant calls "Messianic alienation." It is an experience "that man is not yet, and the faith that he will be, what God means him ultimately to be—which must be experienced by every Jew who enjoys an essential Jewish existence until the final redemption."[7]

V. THE ONGOING PROCESS OF SIFTING AND SEPARATION

"Judaism means to me the election of the seed of Abraham as the nation of God, the imposition upon this people of a series of commandments which express God's will for the conduct of His people and the endless struggle by this people against its election, with the most disastrous consequences to itself as well as the rest of mankind. In spite of all this, the Divine election remains unaffected because it is an unconditional one, not subject to revocation. Lest all this sound inexcusably arrogant, I can only say that indeed it would be, were it the self-election of a people. As it is, it is a sign of God's absolute sovereignty which is not bound by human conceptions of fairness. Israel's election has meant that this people must observe a code of conduct far more difficult than that of any other people and that, when it does not live up to its election, it is visited by pun-

[7]Lionel Rubinoff, in *Judaism* (New York), Fall, 1961.

ishments so terrible that no human justice could ever warrant them."

This participant sees two trends in American Jewish life. On one hand, there are "the 'Jewish' organizations, heavy with money and access to the media of public communication that only money can buy, for whom the Jew's relationship to his God is a topic of very little interest . . . They issue pronouncements on public issues, such as the birth control controversy, without even mentioning the Rabbinic view of the matter, as if the Jewish point of view were self-evidently identical with the ideology of the social sciences or the liberalism of the *New York Post.*"

On the other hand, there is "much that is heartening" in American Jewish life today. "We are witnessing the maturing of a generation . . . in this country . . . , deeply faithful to the Covenant whose level of Jewish literacy would have been inconceivable thirty years ago . . ."[8]

[8]Michael Wyschogrod, in *Judaism* (New York), Fall, 1961.

Part Two

HOW DID JUDAISM REACH ITS PRESENT STATE?

CHAPTER 5

THE EVENTS OF A.D. 70

INTRODUCTION—THE PRIESTLY CHARACTER OF ISRAEL'S
MISSION—A MESSIANIC PROGRAM—A MESSIANIC PERSON—A
MESSIANIC PEOPLE

I. INTRODUCTION

To MANY JEWISH OBSERVERS the present religious state of
the Jewish people is an outgrowth of profound changes in
Jewish life brought about by the political emancipation
which took place some one hundred and fifty years ago.
The emancipation affected primarily the emancipated Jewish communities in Western Europe, but the Jews in
Eastern Europe also came under its influence in the course
of time. The changes mentioned above were related directly to the termination of ghetto conditions and the
gradual submergence of the Jews into the general stream
of the life of the countries of their residence.

Those who attribute all the manifestations of the present
religious state of the Jewish people to the emancipation
are faced with the question, How is it that a religious life
to which Jews clung so tenaciously for some seventeen
centuries began to disintegrate at its first contact with the

outside world? In the State of Israel, where traditional Judaism has shown itself to be incompatible with the functioning of a modern state, sheer necessity makes a thorough study of the religious question imperative. In the Diaspora,[1] where Jewish population constitutes everywhere a small minority, the religious problem does not have the urgency which it has in Israel. Consequently, the approach to this question in the Diaspora lacks the boldness and depth with which it is treated in Israel. Nevertheless, even in the Diaspora there is a serious attempt to come to grips with this problem as evidenced by the two recent religious symposia conducted in America.

As far as this writer is aware, the first satisfactory analysis of the nature of the Jewish religious crisis made by a Jewish observer in the Diaspora is that by Dr. Schoeps, a German Jewish scholar. Referring to the reconstruction of Judaism which followed the cessation of the sacrificial worship, Schoeps writes: "As the Jews of all previous centuries understood it, the great turning point in Jewish history, the first real breach of the historical tradition, was the destruction of the Temple by the Romans under Titus in the year 70 C.E. It is generally agreed that we have the Pharisaic theologians of the time to thank for the fact that this rupture of the historical tradition did not prove fatal and put an end to Jewish history altogether. It was the sages of Jabneh, of Lydda, of Caesarea, and Bene-Brak, who were the first to develop the concept of the 'as if' into an enduring principle of Jewish history. The Theocracy no longer existed, but its constitution remained in force as if it did. The Temple no longer existed, but the Jews the world over bowed in prayer in its direction as if it did. The High Priest no longer made his expiatory sacrifice on

[1]Diaspora—countries of Jewish residence outside of the Land of Israel.

the Day of Atonement, but the ritual formula was learned and recited on that day as if he did. Meanwhile, other things took the place of the actual sacrifice: study of the Torah, good works, prayer—the fulfilling of these commandments counted as much as the animal sacrifice of ancient times.

"This disregard of the actual facts, this abstracting of Judaism from every reality of here and now, was a phenomenal accomplishment. It did indeed 'save' Judaism—that is to say, by means of the 'as if' Judaism was adapted to exile and was removed to the plane of the timeless."[2]

Referring to the effect of the political emancipation in the nineteenth century on Jewish life, Schoeps declares: "Now the thread [of the continuity of Jewish history] was really broken, and the great question that had lain hidden all these years, in the heart of the year 70, first revealed itself for what it really was: the question of Judaism's destiny . . . All those who have not perceived the belated manifestation, commencing about 1800, of the fatality concealed in the year 70, who have not perceived the growing untenability of the 'as if' set down by the sages of Jabneh, will never recognize the right to ask these questions. But it is vital for us that we ask them, for it has ceased to be apparent why the body of the Jewish people should still maintain its separate identity if the individual Jew is going to know as little as he does about the origin (election) and end (God's supremacy) of the Covenant, and its constitutional obligations (Law)."[3]

Now let us recapitulate some of the salient points in Dr.

[2]Hans Joachim Schoeps, "Faith And The Jewish Law Today," in *The Church and the Jewish People*, ed., Gote Hedenquist (London: Edinburgh House Press, 1954), pp. 64-5.
[3]*Ibid.*, pp. 65-6, 67. See also Hans Joachim Schoeps, "How To Live By Jewish Law Today?", *Commentary* (New York), January, 1953.

Schoeps' keen analysis of the events of the year 70. The cessation of the sacrificial worship precipitated a crisis of the first magnitude. The remedy provided by rabbinism was, in Dr. Schoeps' words, an 'as if' remedy, abstracted from every reality. As a matter of fact, this solution was never intended by its authors to be a permanent one; rabbinism never accepted Jewish dispersion and exile as the normal and permanent state of the Jewish people. True, the 'as if' solution lasted for centuries. But this was as much due to external factors as to the intrinsic value of the solution itself. For no sooner did the external factors cease to operate than the 'as if' solution lost its effectiveness.

According to Dr. Schoeps the events of 70, i.e. the cessation of sacrifices, posed the question, What is the destiny of the Jewish people from now on? This question was not answered by the rabbinic reconstruction of Judaism after the year 70. It lay hidden all these centuries, only to rise to the surface under the impact of the emancipation after the year 1800. In other words, the present religious crisis which began after 1800 is the continuation of the religious crisis which was born in the events of the year 70.

In Part Two of this study we wish to discuss: First, in what way did the cessation of the sacrificial worship affect the destiny of the Jewish people? Second, what, if any, is the relation of the messianic movement of Jesus to the events of 70? Finally, if the present religious state of the Jewish people has its real beginning in the events of 70, in what way are certain manifestations of the present religious condition the consequences of the 'as if' rabbinic reconstruction of Judaism?

II. THE PRIESTLY CHARACTER OF ISRAEL'S MISSION

There is a gradual unfolding in the Old Testament of the nature of Israel's mission. It is hinted at in the call of Abraham (Genesis 12:1-3). It appears in sharper outlines in Jacob's farewell blessing before his death (Genesis 49:10). It is unveiled most completely in the prophetic writings. Briefly, Israel's mission is to bring the nations of the earth to God. The sacrificial worship of the Old Testament is designed to teach how God can be approached, and how men and nations, including Israel, can draw near to God. With this in mind, we wish in this chapter to discuss the nature of Israel's mission under the following three headings: A messianic program, a messianic person, and a messianic people.

III. A MESSIANIC PROGRAM

God's redemptive purpose for the world is taught in much of the Old Testament. The following are a few representative passages.

But in the latter days it shall come to pass, that the mountain of Jehovah's house shall be established on the top of the mountains, and it shall be exalted above the hills; and peoples shall flow unto it. And many nations shall go and say, Come ye, and let us go up to the mountain of Jehovah, and to the house of the God of Jacob; and he will teach us of his ways, and we will walk in his paths. For out of Zion shall go forth the law, and the word of Jehovah from Jerusalem; and he will judge between many peoples, and will decide concerning strong nations afar off: and they shall beat their swords into plowshares, and their spears into pruning-hooks; nation shall not lift up sword against nation, neither shall they learn war any more. But they shall sit every man under his vine and under his fig-tree; and none shall make them afraid: for the mouth of Jehovah of hosts hath spoken it.

Micah 4:1-4, A.S.V.

Notice the sequence of events in this prophetic declaration. First, there is Jerusalem, the spiritual center of the world. Second, in this spiritual center a spiritual movement is inaugurated which spreads to many nations in the world. Third, the effect of this spiritual movement set afoot in the world is world peace.

IV. A MESSIANIC PERSON

He is a Descendant of the House of David

And there shall come forth a shoot out of the stock of Jesse, and a branch out of his roots shall bear fruit.

Isaiah 11:1, A.S.V.

He is Israel's King

Behold, the days come, saith Jehovah, that I will raise unto David a righteous Branch, and he shall reign as king and deal wisely, and shall execute justice and righteousness in the land. In his days Judah shall be saved, and Israel shall dwell safely; and this is his name whereby he shall be called: Jehovah our righteousness.

Jeremiah 23:5-6, A.S.V.

He is the God-Man

This has already been indicated in the above scriptural passage—a King of the Davidic dynasty whose name shall be Jehovah our righteousness. The same thought is stated in the following lines from Isaiah:

For unto us a child is born, unto us a son is given; and the government shall be upon his shoulder: and his name shall be called Wonderful, Counsellor, Mighty God, Everlasting Father, Prince of Peace.

                                                Isaiah 9:6, A.S.V.

His Qualifications

And the Spirit of Jehovah shall rest upon him, the spirit of wisdom and understanding, the spirit of counsel and might, the spirit of knowledge and of the fear of Jehovah.

                                                Isaiah 11:2, A.S. V

His Mission

He will execute justice.

And he shall not judge after the sight of his eyes, neither decide after the hearing of his ears; but with righteousness shall he judge the poor, and decide with equity for the meek of the earth; and he shall smite the earth with the rod of his mouth; and with the breath of his lips shall he slay the wicked.

                                                Isaiah 11:3-4, A.S.V.

He will tame human nature.

And the wolf shall dwell with the lamb, and the leopard shall lie down with the kid; and the calf and the young lion and the fatling together; and a little child shall lead them. . . . They shall not hurt nor destroy in all my holy mountain; for the earth shall be full of the knowledge of Jehovah, as the waters cover the sea.

                                                Isaiah 11:6, 9, A.S.V.

He will be the rallying center for all nations.

And it shall come to pass in that day, that the root of Jesse, that standeth for an ensign [or banner] of the peoples, unto him shall the nations seek; . . .

                                                Isaiah 11:10, A.S.V.

The burden of the above scriptural teachings is that the messianic program will be headed up by a messianic person. And while judgment is meted out on the wicked, world peace is achieved not by force but by the transformation of human nature and the worldwide diffusion of the knowledge of Jehovah.

V. A MESSIANIC PEOPLE

Israel is the messianic people whose mission is to win the nations to God, under the direction of her messianic king.

> This people have I formed for myself, they shall show forth [declare] my praise.
>
> Isaiah 43:21

This divine purpose of the election and mission of Israel was revealed simultaneously with the call of Abraham.

> Now Jehovah said unto Abram, get thee out of thy country, and from thy kindred, and from thy father's house, unto the land that I will show thee: and I will make of thee a great nation, and I will bless thee, and make thy name great; and be thou a blessing: and I will bless them that bless thee, and him that curseth thee will I curse: and in thee shall all the families of the earth be blessed.
>
> Genesis 12:1-3, A.S.V.

This declaration that Israel shall be a blessing to all the nations of the earth was repeated to Isaac (Genesis 26:4), and to Jacob (Genesis 28:14).

This mission of Israel was for the first time disclosed to the whole nation in the third month after its departure from Egypt. In fact, this mission was the real purpose of Israel's deliverance from Egypt.

Ye have seen what I did unto the Egyptians, and how I bare you on eagles' wings, and brought you unto myself. Now therefore, if ye will obey my voice indeed, and keep my covenant, then ye shall be mine own possession from among all peoples: for all the earth is mine: and ye shall be unto me a kingdom of priests, and a holy nation . . .

Exodus 19:4-6, A.S.V.

"God is the Creator of all things and the Father of all mankind. Israel, in common with every other nation, forms part of God's possession; but He has chosen Israel to be His in a special degree, to be 'a light unto the nations' and a blessing to all humanity. There is no thought of favouritism in God's choice. Israel's call has not been to privilege and rulership, but to martyrdom and service . . . As it is the duty of the priest to bring man nearer to God, so Israel has been called to play the part of a priest to other nations; i.e. to bring them closer to God and Righteousness."[4]

But a priest could not begin his priestly functions until he had been consecrated to his office, until he had been, so to speak, made holy. Chapters 28 and 29 of Exodus give a detailed description of the ritual connected with the consecration of a priest. It was a ritual in which sin and burnt offerings were sacrificed and the blood sprinkled upon the altar and the priest.

As with the individual priest, so with the priestly nation. Israel must be consecrated before she can assume the duties of her mission to the nations. Before she can bring the nations near to God, she herself must come near to God. Before she can preach holiness to the nations of the earth, she must first become holy herself. The passage in Exodus

[4] J. H. Hertz, late Chief Rabbi of Great Britain, *The Pentateuch and Haftorahs* (London: Soncino Press, 1938), pp. 291-2.

19:4-6, cited above, points to the instrument by which
Israel will become that holy nation. That instrument is
the Covenant: "If ye will obey my voice indeed, and keep
my covenant." The keeping of the Covenant will place
Israel in a special relationship to God, in consequence of
which she will acquire holiness.

At the heart of the Covenant is the institution of sacrifices. The Abrahamic Covenant, which is the basis of the
Sinai Covenant, was made by means of a sacrifice (Genesis
15:9-18) ; and the Sinai Covenant with the nation of Israel
was also made with a sacrifice, half of the blood of which
was sprinkled upon the altar and the other half upon the
people (Exodus 24:3-8). Not only this, but the conclusion
of the Sinai Covenant was followed by the institution of
the elaborate Old Testament sacrificial cult, whose object
was to maintain the Covenant relationship between God
and Israel.

There was a variety of sacrifices, and they differed from
one another in substance, in the manner in which they
were offered, and in the names which they bore. They
were designed to meet a variety of human needs. However,
there was one name which was used to designate all kinds
of offerings, and this name is the Hebrew word "Korban,"
derived from the verb "Karab." "Karab" means "to approach," "to come near." The hiphil form of "Karab" is
"Hikrib" which means "to cause to come near." In its
broader sense "Korban" includes even offerings not placed
on the altar, such as the firstfruits, gold, silver, and wood
(Leviticus 2:12; Numbers 7:3, 12; 31:50; Nehemiah 10:34;
13:31). God being holy and man being of a sinful nature,
man could never in the Old Testament approach God until
a life was sacrificed on the altar as an atonement for man's
sins. It was this bloody sacrifice that determined man's

entire relationship to God. Without this bloody sacrifice there is no access to God under the Sinai Covenant, either for the individual Israelite or the nation Israel.

However precious were the truths embodied in the sacrificial cult of the Old Testament, the animal sacrifice was an imperfect representation of these truths. The animal's life was inferior to that of man. Consequently, such a life could hardly be a substitute for human sin. The animal is not a moral, and therefore not a holy, being. The animal is not a willing sacrifice. It was therefore not possible for animal sacrifices to bring real forgiveness of sins or be the means of union between God and man. It was chiefly due to the labors of Israel's prophets that men came to see that the chief function of the Old Testament sacrifices was to produce and deepen in man a sense of God's holiness and man's sinfulness, and to point to the coming of the perfect Servant of Jehovah, by whom and in whom all human needs, expressed but never met by the animal sacrifices, will be truly and perfectly satisfied. There is a whole body of teachings in the Old Testament concerning the Servant of Jehovah. The following are a few representative passages:

The Servant of Jehovah.

The Servant of Jehovah is a sinless and righteous being.

Behold the days come, saith Jehovah, that I will raise unto David a righteous Branch, . . . and this is his name whereby he shall be called: Jehovah our righteousness.

Jeremiah 23:5-6, A.S.V.

The Servant of Jehovah is a suffering servant.

He was despised, and rejected of men; a man of sorrows, and acquainted with grief.

Isaiah 53:3, A.S.V.

The Servant of Jehovah is an innocent sufferer.

. . . he had done no violence, neither was any deceit in his mouth.

Isaiah 53:9, A.S.V.

The Servant of Jehovah is a willing sufferer.

He was oppressed, yet when he was afflicted he opened not his mouth; as a lamb that is led to the slaughter, and as a sheep that before its shearers is dumb, so he opened not his mouth.

Isaiah 53:7, A.S.V.

The Servant of Jehovah suffers for the sins of Israel.

But he was wounded for our transgressions, he was bruised for our iniquities; the punishment was laid on him for our well-being.

Isaiah 53:5

The Servant of Jehovah dies for the sins of Israel.

. . . he was cut off out of the land of the living for the transgression of my people to whom the stroke was due. . . . he poured out his soul unto death.

Isaiah 53:8, 12, A.S.V.

And they made his grave with the wicked.

Isaiah 53:9, A.S.V.

The Servant of Jehovah is the great Sin-bearer and Intercessor.

. . . he bare the sin of many, and made [maketh] intercession for the transgressors.

Isaiah 53:12, A.S.V.

Though the immediate result of human action, the

death of the Servant of Jehovah was predetermined by God
to become the means of man's redemption.

> . . . and Jehovah hath laid on him the iniquity of us
> all. Yet it pleased Jehovah to bruise him; he hath put
> him to grief; when his soul shall make an offering for sin,
> he shall see seed, he shall prolong his days, and the pleas-
> ure [i.e. the purpose] of Jehovah shall prosper through
> his hand.
>
> Isaiah 53:6, 10

The Servant of Jehovah is the Mediator of a new Covenant.

> Behold, my servant, whom I uphold; my chosen, in
> whom my soul delighteth: I have put my Spirit upon him;
> he will bring forth justice to the Gentiles. I, Jehovah,
> have called thee in righteousness, and will hold thy hand,
> and will keep thee, and give thee for a covenant of the
> people, for a light of the Gentiles.
>
> Isaiah 42:1, 6, A.S.V.

The Targum begins the first sentence of this prophetic
passage thus: "Behold, my servant Messiah," etc., etc.
According to Jeremiah, the Covenant of which Messiah
will be the Mediator will be a New Covenant, not like the
Sinai Covenant.

> Behold, the days come, saith Jehovah, that I will make
> a new covenant with the house of Israel, and with the
> house of Judah: not according to the covenant that I
> made with their fathers in the day that I took them by
> the hand to bring them out of the land of Egypt; which
> my covenant they brake, although I was a husband unto
> them, saith Jehovah. But this is the covenant that I will
> make with the house of Israel after those days, saith Je-
> hovah: I will put my law in their inward parts, and in

their heart will I write it; and I will be their God, and
they shall be my people. And they shall teach no more
every man his neighbor, and every man his brother, saying, Know Jehovah; for they shall all know me, from
the least of them unto the greatest of them, saith Jehovah:
for I will forgive their iniquity, and their sin will I remember no more.

Jeremiah 31:31-34, A.S.V. (31:30-33 Heb.)

The making of this New Covenant with Israel will mark
the end of Israel's training for her mission, a training
which began in the wilderness after the exodus from Egypt.
Israel will at last have become a holy nation, ready to assume her priestly duties among the nations of the earth
under the leadership of her messianic King.

And it shall come to pass, that he that is left in Zion,
and he that remaineth in Jerusalem, shall be called holy,
even every one that is written among the living in Jerusalem; when the Lord shall have washed away the filth
of the daughter of Zion, and shall have purged the blood
of Jerusalem from the midst thereof, by the spirit of
justice, and by the spirit of burning.

Isaiah 4:3-4, A.S.V.

CHAPTER 6

THE MESSIANIC MOVEMENT OF JESUS OF NAZARETH

THE DESTRUCTION OF THE TEMPLE, with the cessation of Israel's sacrificial worship, was the event in the first century which precipitated a crisis in the religious destiny of the Jewish people. There was another event in the first century which—at least from this writer's point of view—was related to the catastrophe which befell the Jewish people at the end of the first and beginning of the second century, and to the subsequent rabbinic reconstruction of Israel's religion. That event was the emergence of the messianic movement of Jesus of Nazareth. Modern Jewish scholarship acknowledges that the New Testament contains trustworthy facts about the life and work of Jesus. Among His contemporary opponents there was no agreement as to who He was, but they fully agreed that He was an extraordinary person. The few reliable bits of information about Him in Jewish rabbinic writings confirm the New Testament reports that He possessed healing powers and that even His disciples after the crucifixion exercised healing powers in His name.[1] He displayed an unusual insight into the meaning of the Scriptures. He taught as one having authority. He had a deep consciousness of His messianic mission to Israel and to the world.

Israel's national restoration held a central place in Jewish messianic expectancies. It was uppermost in the minds and hearts of the disciples of Jesus. From the beginning

[1]B. Abodah Zarah 27b. Compare also Tosefta-Hullin 22, 23; P. Shabbath 14d; P. Abodah Zarah 40d, 41a.

to the end of His earthly ministry they expected that He would expel the Romans and set up a politically independent Jewish state in Palestine. To Jesus, Israel's spiritual redemption was of prime importance and had to come first. "Seek ye first his [God's] kingdom, and his righteousness," He told Israel, "and all these things shall be added unto you" (Matthew 6:33). One would suppose that the state of affairs under the monarchy in the days of the first Temple, as recorded in the historical books of the Old Testament, and the experiences under the Maccabean monarchy in the days of the second Temple, would have exercised a sobering effect on the contemporaries of Jesus and caused His words to fall on receptive hearts. But alas! Jerusalem of that day had not known the things which belonged to her peace; they were hidden from her eyes (Luke 19:42). When it became evident to the disciples that Jesus was headed for the cross instead of for the crown, their messianic movement began to show signs of dissolution.

But the empty tomb on Sunday morning after the crucifixion was the turning point in the lives of the disciples and the turning point in the history of the world. In the forty days which followed the resurrection the risen Christ was seen by the apostles and about five hundred other disciples. The resurrection of Jesus changed them from timid followers into fearless apostles with a message of salvation for the whole world. In the light of the crucifixion and the resurrection they reread the Old Testament Scriptures and saw the world's sin from the point of view of a righteous, holy, compassionate, and forgiving God. They now fully realized that the kingdom of God could never have been established on earth apart from the regeneration of men's hearts and their evil nature.

As they pondered on the mystery of the Cross
On which their beloved Lord had died,
All they were, and all they had, they counted loss
And poured contempt on all their pride.

In the thirty-seven years which followed the crucifixion and resurrection, apostolic Hebrew Christianity went up and down the land of Israel, proclaiming the Gospel of reconciliation. The apostles declared to their people that the death of Jesus the Messiah had taken place in accordance with the predetermined counsel of God in order that through Messiah's atoning death all men should find forgiveness for their sins. They assured their people that if they would turn to God in true repentance and surrender their hearts to Messiah Jesus, God would pour out upon them the full measure of His blessings and fulfill through them His redemptive purpose for all mankind.

Had Israel heeded the message of first century Hebrew Christianity, the catastrophe of A.D. 70 might have been prevented, the slaughter of hundreds of thousands of Jews and the desolation of the land of Israel could have been avoided, the Jewish people would have remained in their land, and the subsequent centuries of world history would have had a different story to tell. But Israel let that great day of opportunity pass. She thus proved that she was not yet fully prepared for her world mission. Therefore she was returned to the wilderness, "the wilderness of the peoples [nations]" (Ezekiel 20:35, A.S.V.), there to complete her training, even as the generation which had left Egypt and stood on the border of Canaan within sight and reach of the Promised Land had demonstrated its unreadiness to take possession of its inheritance, and was sent back into the wilderness of the Exodus.

CHAPTER 7

THE DRIFT AWAY FROM THE BIBLE

WORKS VERSUS FAITH—THE EXALTATION OF THE TORAH—THE DOWNGRADING OF THE BIBLE—THE DEPERSONALIZATION OF GOD—THE DEPERSONALIZATION OF THE MESSIAH—CONCLUDING OBSERVATIONS ON THE CAUSE OF THE JEWISH SPIRITUAL DILEMMA

I. WORKS VERSUS FAITH

THE CESSATION of the sacrificial worship in the first century disrupted the divinely instituted approach to God. The Jewish followers of Jesus saw in this event indirect proof that the atoning death of the Messiah had made the continuation of the Old Testament sacrificial cult unnecessary. Having said no to the messianic claims of Jesus, Jewish religious leadership was hard put to find a theological explanation for the events of A.D. 70. The chief sin which brought about the destruction of the first Temple was idolatry. But there was no idolatry in the days of the second Temple. There is a passage in the Talmud which states that it was the sin of "hatred without a cause" which led to the destruction of the second Temple, because—it is explained—the sin of "hatred without a cause" is equivalent to the combined effect of the sins of idolatry, incest, and murder.[1] It is quite possible that this represents an isolated opinion; otherwise it could have easily played into the hands of the followers of Jesus, especially in view of the fact that in the Gospel of John "hatred without a cause" is mentioned as one of the factors which led to the Jewish rejection of Jesus (John 15:25).

This only goes to show how the very existence of the Christian faith must have proved an embarrassment to religious Judaism. Having originated in the Holy Land and in the bosom of the Old Testament religion, Christianity looked upon itself as the goal to which the Old Testament pointed. It challenged religious Judaism to justify from the pages of the Old Testament its opposition to Jesus Christ.

Thus it was that under the combined influence of these two farreaching developments—the cessation of the Old Testament sacrificial worship and the Christian challenge —Judaism was steered in a direction away from the Bible. It is true that this rabbinic trend was in evidence even before A.D. 70. But the existence of the Temple cult with its powerful priesthood acted as a brake on this rabbinic trend. The cessation of the sacrificial worship removed the priesthood as an influential force from Jewish life. Rabbinism was thus left free to pursue its course.

And yet rabbinism fulfilled an important historical mission. With the loss of the Jewish national homeland a substitute had to be provided to safeguard Jewish nationality. Rabbinism produced this safeguard by creating a uniform religious way of life which served to cement unity between the Jewish communities dispersed all over the world. Humanly speaking, rabbinism saved Jewish nationality from

[1]Yoma 9b.

extinction. It built a spiritual fence around the Jew which together with the physical wall erected by the Gentiles around the ghetto served to seal the Jew off effectively from outside influence. This will explain the seemingly strange phenomenon that when the ghetto walls were removed following the Napoleonic wars and the Jew became exposed to the outside world the spiritual fence of rabbinism began to fall apart. This gave rise to the nineteenth century phase of the religious crisis which has lasted to this day and for which there appears to be no solution. The primary elements of the present phase of the religious crisis have their roots in the two events in Jewish life which took place in the first century—the cessation of the sacrificial cult and the emergence of the messianic movement of Jesus. The secondary elements of the present crisis are the end results of the anti-Biblical tendencies which, consciously or unconsciously, rabbinism pursued in its efforts to solve the first century phase of the religious crisis. The primary factors have been described above. We will now proceed with a discussion of the secondary factors of the present phase of the Jewish religious crisis.

If the reader will now turn to Part One of this study or the two periodicals which conducted the symposia, he will see that many of the participants stress the fact that Judaism favors deeds over faith. "I do not regard Jewishness as primarily a matter of religious belief. The most profound and valuable insight of Judaic religion was, I believe, the ideal of universal justice. . . ."[2] "Knowledge and action are paramount over faith."[3] "Torah and mitzvah—reverence for learning and the piety of the 'deed,' of 'right action'—were the constant factors in Jewish exist-

[2]Raziel Abelson, in *Commentary* (New York), April, 1961.
[3]Enoch Gordis, in *Commentary* (New York), April, 1961.

ence."[4] "I find compelling in this ethic [of Judaism of the last 1,000 years][5] . . . its conviction that redemption lies within the grasp of any man, not through 'faith' but through his assumption of the responsibility of being his brother's keeper . . .[6] Notice also the following utterances culled from other sources: "Moreover, Judaism places the emphasis on practical religion rather than on dogma."[7] "Whereas Christianity emphasizes salvation by grace, Judaism stresses salvation through works."[8]

Modern Jewish orthodoxy demands unquestioned adherence to the Law. "It is not true, then, that Judaism is a 'religion of law' . . . It is law, pure and simple, accepted by the Jewish nation at Mount Sinai . . . Judaism, in contrast [to other religions], demands actions, irrespective of convictions . . . Judaism does not—in the manner of religions—aim to gain acceptance by 'convincing' the individual but by giving him, as the member of a nation, historical self-consciousness . . . It is not faith, then, which redeems the Jew, but historical self-consciousness. . . ."[9]

Though Liberal Judaism gave up belief in the divine origin of the Law, its position on the importance of the Law in Jewish religious life is the same as that of Orthodox Judaism, as seen from the following excerpts:

"It is not so much what man's belief is, but how that belief expresses itself in conduct."[10] Faith in Judaism we

[4]Israel Knox, in *Judaism* (New York), Fall, 1961.
[5]Of 1000 years of Ashkenazi Judaism.
[6]Joseph C. Landis, in *Judaism* (New York), Fall, 1961.
[7]Cecil Roth (ed.), *The Standard Jewish Encyclopedia* (Garden City, N. Y.: Doubleday & Co., 1959), p. 1078.
[8]Ernst Jacob, in *Universal Jewish Encyclopedia* (New York: The Universal Jewish Encyclopedia, Inc., 1939, vol. 3, p. 186.
[9]Isaac Breuer, *The Problem of the Jew* (New York: The Spero Foundation, 1947), pp. 61, 63, 58.
[10]Rabbi Abba Hillel Silver, *Where Judaism Differed* (New York: The Macmillan Co., 1956), p. 173.

are told by the same Rabbinical writer, is not a creed in the accepted sense of the word, but an adherence to a code of moral practice revealed to man.[11]

"All radiates from the Law, and from it all depends."[12]

"Only the right deed places man in the presence of God at all times and only it can be demanded of him at all times. Through it alone can man reach that deep inner unity with God, as well as that other unity with his fellow men. . . . Judaism also has its Word, but it is only one word—'to do.' "[13]

This works-versus-faith attitude, which is so characteristic of present-day Judaism, is the final stage in the evolution of a religious trend. This trend had its inception in the beginning of the Christian era. It was Rabbinic Judaism's answer to the doctrinal position of the New Testament, epitomized in Paul's declaration that "by the works of the law shall no flesh be justified in his sight" (Letter to the Romans 3:20).[14] It led to the exaltation of the Law by rabbinism as seen from the following few but representative passages from Talmudic writings.

II. THE EXALTATION OF THE TORAH

In its narrow sense Torah refers to the Law of Moses, or the written Law. In its broad sense "Torah" includes the whole of the Old Testament and also the so-called oral Law. By "oral law" is meant a body of rabbinic literature which we now call the Talmud. It consists of two parts, the Mishnah, which was compiled in written form

[11]*Ibid.*, p. 174.
[12]C. G. Montefiore, "Rabbinic Judaism and the Epistles of St. Paul," *Journal Quarterly Review*, XIII (1901), 173.
[13]Leo Baeck, *The Essence of Judaism* (New York: Shocken Books, 1948), p. 56. Copyright 1948 by Schocken Books, Inc., New York. Quoted by permission.
[14]"Justified in his sight"—declared righteous in the sight of God.

at the end of the third century of the Christian era, and the Gemarah, which is a commentary on the Mishnah and was compiled toward the end of the fifth century. The name "oral Law" is derived from the fact that for a long time it existed by virtue of oral transmission. Rabbinism taught that this oral Law was given to Moses by God at the same time as the written Law, and that from Moses this unwritten Law was passed on together with the written Law to Joshua; Joshua delivered it to the elders; the elders to the prophets; and the prophets passed this tradition on to the Men of the Great Assembly,[15] a religious institution which is said to have arisen in the days of Ezra, in accordance with the record contained in Nehemiah, chapters 8 to 10.[16] The Great Assembly, or as it is also called, the Great Synagogue, is the ancestor of traditional Rabbinic Judaism.

The Torah existed before the creation of the world.[17]

The Torah participated in the creation of the world. In creating the world God was guided by the Torah as an architect is guided by his blueprint when planning the construction of some edifice.[18]

The world was created for the sake of the Torah.[19]

The Torah is Israel's Mediator.[20]

The Torah is unchangeable. No other Moses will come to bring another Torah, for there is no other Torah left in Heaven.[21] The anti-New Testament connotation of the

[15]Pirkē Abot 1:1.
[16]See, George Foot Moore, *Judaism in the First Centuries of the Christian Era* (Cambridge: Harvard University Press, 1927), Vol. I, chap. 2.
[17]Abot 6:10.
[18]Midrash Gen. R. 1:2; 3:5.
[19]Midrash Gen. R. 12:2.
[20]Midrash Ex. R. 29:3.
[21]Midrash Dt. R. 8:6. In Part Three of this study we have a statement from a work by a scholarly religious Israeli Jew to the effect that the prophets of the Old Testament definitely teach that in the messianic era there will be a new divine revelation.

68 *The Spiritual Dilemma of the Jewish People*

above statement is evident when compared with the following passage in the Gospel of John: "For the law was given by Moses, but grace and truth came by Jesus Christ" (John 1:17).

In the third chapter of his letter to the Romans Paul discusses the matter of Abraham's justification by faith as recorded in the fifteenth chapter of Genesis. This statement in Genesis, that Abraham was considered righteous in the sight of God on the basis of his trust in God, is recorded before the Abrahamic Covenant was made and some time before the commandment of circumcision was given. To this the rabbinic answer was that the patriarchs observed the written and even the unwritten Law, notwithstanding the fact that the patriarchs lived cenuries before the promulgation of the written law.[22]

Side by side with the emphasis of present-day Judaism on works versus faith there is a tendency to divorce ethical conduct from religion or faith in God. To be sure, this tendency is not confined to Judaism alone. "I have no quarrel with religion for others: I believe I have a strong sense of ethics and social responsibility without it."[23] One American rabbi states that Jews can no longer accept on intellectual grounds a belief in a personal God. He, therefore, calls for the creation of a Jewish humanism which would be concerned not with God but with humanity.[24] In a pamphlet seeking to explain the aims of the Jewish reconstructionist movement, we are told that religion should not be viewed as a supernaturally revealed creed or code but rather as the affirmation of the worthwhileness

[22]Sifre Dt. par. 345. Tanchuma Lek Leka par. 1; also Yoma 28 b.
[23]Arnold M. Rose, in *Judaism* (New York), Fall, 1961.
[24]Richard M. Leviton, "Jewish Humanism," *Jewish Spectator* (New York), September, 1960.

of life.[25] This is the extreme logical development of the idealization and idolization of ethical conduct. If man's salvation is determined by his conduct rather than by his relation to God, then man can save himself and God can be dispensed with. This tendency to separate man's ethical conduct from faith in God, or the Law from God, may be seen in the following Talmudic passages:

"Would that they [the Jewish people] would forsake Me but keep My Torah."[26]

One of the Talmudic sages who represented a minority opinion in a discussion of a certain halachah (i.e. legal item) appealed to Heaven for a decision. The voice which came from Heaven in response to this appeal gave its support to the dissenting rabbi. But this heavenly decision was promptly set aside by the deliberating rabbis representing the majority opinion. This action was justified on the grounds that since the Torah was delivered by God to Israel, the consensus of rabbinic opinion carries more weight than a voice from Heaven.[27]

The great Rabbi Hillel the Elder has for many centuries exerted a powerful influence on traditional Judaism. The story is told that a heathen asked him once to teach him the Law while standing on one foot; in other words, he wished Hillel to tell him what is the essence of the Jewish religion. The answer which Hillel gave is as follows: "Do not do to your fellow that which is hateful to you. This is the whole Law. The rest is its interpretation."[28] Not a word about faith in God or man's relationship to God!

[25]Hannah L. Goldberg, *Introduction to Reconstructionism* (New York: The Jewish Reconstructionist Foundation, 1945), p. 15.
[26]J. Hag. 1:7.
[27]Baba Mezia 59b.
[28]Shabbath 31 a.

Of course, this exaltation of the Law by rabbinism is not quite in agreement with the teachings of the Old Testament. The Ten Commandments which represent the first body of laws given on Mount Sinai begin not with a commandment, but with a divine declaration. In this declaration God defines His relationship to Israel, based on what He has done for Israel, and not on what the Israelites have done for Him. "I am Jehovah thy God, who brought thee out of the land of Egypt, out of the house of bondage" (Exodus 20:2).

As for Israel, she has broken the Law through her entire Biblical history: in the wilderness, and in the days of the first Temple. And since the Synagogue recognizes that the catastrophe of the year 70 was due to Israel's sinfulness, this means that Israel broke the Law in the days of the second Temple also.

Not only so, but Moses, Aaron, and their sister Miriam —these three under whose leadership the Exodus from Egypt had taken place—all failed before God in the wilderness. Aaron, Israel's first high priest, transgressed and was appointed to die in the wilderness and be buried there. His two sons died because of their sins. And Moses, who in the Old Testament stands nearer to God than any other human being, was not permitted to enter the promised land because of failure to comply with God's will, and he too was left to die in the wilderness. And it is this broken Sinai Covenant that God promised through Jeremiah to replace, and to replace it, not with another Covenant of Law but with a New Covenant of grace (Jeremiah 31:31-34 [31:30-33, Heb.]). Thus we can see that Paul stood on Old Testament ground when he declared that "by the works of the law shall no flesh be justified" (Letter to the Romans 3:20).

III. THE DOWNGRADING OF THE BIBLE

Rabbinism was not unaware that its teachings were not always in harmony with the Bible. This may be seen from a reference in the Mishnah to the effect that important parts of Rabbinic law are like "mountains hanging by a hair,"[29] i.e., find little support in the Biblical text. Perhaps this awareness led to a gradual depreciation of the Bible, as seen from the following excerpts:

"The Rabbis have taught, that when Rabbi Eliezer was ill, his disciples came to visit him, and they said to him, 'Rabbi, teach us the ways of life that we may merit eternal life.' His answer, among other things, was: 'Prevent your children from meditating.' That he referred to meditating upon Scripture is seen from Rashi's comment on this passage: 'Do not get your children accustomed to read the Bible too much, so that they may not be carried away by it.'"[30]

"Our Rabbis taught, that to be engaged in the study of the Bible is neither good nor bad, but to be engaged in the study of the Mishnah is a good habit and it brings reward, while there is nothing better than the study of the Gemara."[31]

"My son, give heed to the words of the Scribes rather than the words of the Law [i.e. the Law of Moses], for the words of the Law consist of positive and negative precepts [the transgression of which is not always a capital offense]; but whosoever transgresses any of the words of the Scribes is guilty of death."[32]

"It is a more serious matter to contradict the words of

[29]Hagigah 1:8.
[30]Berakoth 28b.
[31]Baba Mezia 33a ("Mishnah" and "Gemara"—the two main divisions of the Talmud).
[32]Erubin 21b.

the Scribes [Mishnah] than the words of the Law of Moses."[33]

". . . He who interprets the Law [of Moses] not according to Halachah [i.e. in the manner of the rabbis], even though he possesses [the virtue of the knowledge of] Torah and good deeds has no portion in the world to come."[34] This statement is attributed to Rabbi Eleazar. He was a member of the assembly at Yabneh which under the presidency of Rabbi Gamaliel was busy reconstructing Judaism following the cessation of the sacrificial cult. Rabbi Gamaliel was the one at whose request the test prayer, the so-called Birkat Haminim, was composed, which contained a curse upon heretics, mainly Hebrew Christians. Rabbi Eleazar's saying cited above belongs to the same circle of ideas and was probably aimed at Hebrew Christians, since at that time only Hebrew Christians were likely to interpret the Law of Moses not according to the Halachah. "The [rabbinic] sage is more important than the prophet."[35]

IV. THE DEPERSONALIZATION OF GOD

The Old Testament is frankly anthropomorphic, i.e., it ascribes to God human form or human qualities. By anthropopathism is meant the imputation to God of human feelings or emotions, such as love, anger, displeasure, etc. There is a rabbinic saying to the effect that the Torah speaks the language of man, i.e., in His effort to communicate with man God adopts human ways. This is certainly correct; there could be no divine revelation unless God condescended to use human means by which to make Himself and His will known to man. But this is not all. Biblical anthropopathism reflects a truth which is basic in Bib-

[33] Sanhedrin 11:3; Yebamoth 89b-90a.
[34] Abot 3:15. See comment on this passage by R. Travers Herford, in *Pirkē Abot* (New York: Jewish Institute of Religion, 1945), pp. 81-82.
[35] Baba Batra 12a.

lical theology, namely, that the same God who is everywhere, in, outside, and beyond His creation, is also the personal God of mankind.

The first definite attempt to weaken this Old Testament concept of a personal God may be seen in the Septuagint, which is the name of a Greek translation of the Old Testament made in Alexandria, Egypt. There is no agreement as to the exact date of the completion of this translation, but it is believed that the Pentateuch was translated first, about the middle of the third century before the Christian era, while the other parts of the Old Testament were translated at a later date. Alexandria had a large and prosperous Jewish community, and the mother tongue of the Jews there was Greek. A great need was felt by the Alexandrian Jews to have the Bible, especially the Pentateuch which was read in the synagogues, in their own tongue. The elimination of many of the anthropomorphic expressions from the Greek Septuagint was prompted by a desire to adapt it to the Greek way of thinking of the Alexandrian Jews. The following are a few examples.

And upon the nobles of the children of Israel he [God] laid not his hand (Hebrew)

And of the elect of Israel not one uttered a dissenting voice (Septuagint)

Exodus 24:11

And there I [God] will meet with thee (Hebrew)

And thence I will be known to thee (Septuagint)

Exodus 25:22

And I [God] will dwell in the midst of the children of Israel (Hebrew)

And I will be invoked by the children of Israel (Septuagint)

Exodus 29:45

The eternal God is a dwelling-place (Hebrew)
The power of God will protect thee (Septuagint)

Deuteronomy 33:27.[36]

The Septuagint reflects Greek influence and an effort to bring Old Testament ideas in accord with Greek philosophy. This development reached its climax in Philo, a Greek Jewish philosopher, of Alexandria, who lived at the end of the first century before Christ and in the first half of the first century of the Christian era. In Philo's philosophy God became so transcendent that He practically became unknowable.

While rabbinism of the Aramaic-speaking Palestinian Jews had no need to harmonize Old Testament ideas with Greek thought, it, in time, was confronted with such a need by the challenge presented to it by the rise of the Christian faith. Targum Onkelos is the name of an Aramaic translation of the Pentateuch which appeared among the Aramaic-speaking Jews of Palestine in the second century of the Christian era. From its very inception it has exercised considerable authority in traditional Judaism. To this day many Hebrew Bibles print the Targum Onkelos version alongside the Hebrew text of the Pentateuch. This Targum version shows a definite tendency to eliminate certain anthropomorphic ideas of the Hebrew text, impelled to do this by a necessity to counteract the doctrine of the Incarnation of the New Testament. The following are a few illustrations:

And Jehovah went his way, as soon as he left off speaking to Abraham. (Hebrew)

[36]See *The Septuagint Bible*, by Charles Thomson (Indian Hills, Colo.: The Falcon's Wing Press, 1945); also, Charlest T. Fritsch, *The Anti-Anthropomorphisms of the Greek Pentateuch* (Princeton, N. J.: Princeton University Press, 1943).

And the Glory of Jehovah departed when he had ceased
to speak with Abraham. (Targum)

Genesis 18:33

And, behold, Jehovah stood above it. (Hebrew)
And, behold, the Glory of Jehovah stood above it.
(Targum)

Genesis 28:13

And, behold, I am with thee. (Hebrew)
And, behold, My Word shall be for thy help. (Targum)

Genesis 28-15

I [Jehovah] have surely seen the affliction of my people
that are in Egypt . . .; for I know their sorrows. (Hebrew)
The bondage of my people which is in Egypt is verily
disclosed before Me . . .; for their afflictions are disclosed
before Me. (Targum)

Exodus 3:7

This last sentence deserves some comment. In the Hebrew text God states: "I know their sorrows." In the Targum their sorrows are merely disclosed before God. The "I know" in the Hebrew text does not refer to being aware of the afflictions of Israel. An Omniscient God would be expected to be aware of everything which transpires on this earth. The expression "I know" in the Hebrew version has the connotation of intimate knowledge, bordering on personal experience. We have here the beginning of one of the most precious teachings of the Bible, namely, that God identifies Himself with His people's joys and sorrows. This may be seen from the following passages: "And his [God's] soul was grieved for the misery of Israel" (Judges 10:16) . "In all their afflictions he [God]

was afflicted, and the angel of his presence saved them"
(Isaiah 63:9). This concept reaches its culmination in the
teachings concerning the suffering Servant of Jehovah
through whom God is willing to identify Himself with His
people in their sins, sickness, and death (Isaiah 53).

To return now to the question of the depersonalization
of God in rabbinic Judaism. The following statements in
the *Universal Jewish Encyclopedia* are of importance.

> The doctrine of divine attributes played a great role
> in the Christian doctrine of the trinity; it was in connec-
> tion with such theological discussions between Christians
> and Mohammedans that the Mutakallimum (Moham-
> medan rationalist theologians of the 8th and following
> centuries) developed the doctrine of divine attributes
> which is so important in medieval Jewish philosophy.
> The Jewish philosophers from Saadia to Albo (10th to
> 15th centuries) and beyond followed in the main the
> discussions of the Arabs.[37]

> In Palestine and Babylonia, however, no progress [in
> the depersonalization of God] was made until the begin-
> ning of the philosophic movement with Saadia (10th
> cent.). From Saadia to Albo (15th cent.) the elimination
> of anthropomorphism was one of the motives of the doc-
> trine of the attributes, and Maimonides (12th cent.) was
> not far behind Philo in insisting on the absolute tran-
> scendence of God . . . The modern Jewish view is the
> same as that of the philosophers.[38]

V. THE DEPERSONALIZATION OF THE MESSIAH

In the middle of the nineteenth century newly formed
Liberal Judaism in Germany took steps to introduce certain

[37]Isaac Husik, "Attributes of God," *The Universal Jewish Encyclopedia*
(New York: The Universal Jewish Encyclopedia, Inc. 1939), I, 609.
[38]"Anthropomorphism," article in *The Universal Jewish Encyclopedia*
(New York), I, 334-5.

important changes in the ritual of the Synagogue. Among other things it decided to delete from the Prayer Book all references to a national restoration of the Jews to Zion, as well as references to the coming of the Messiah. In place of "Redeemer" the word "Redemption" was substituted. For the first time in many centuries Jews in the emancipated countries of Western Europe began to feel at home in the countries of their birth or residence. The petitions for a national restoration to Palestine lost all meaning to them. Since the hope of national restoration to Zion and the coming of the Messiah are closely related in the Jewish religion, the idea of a Messiah was discarded along with the hope of national restoration. However, subsequent events proved how wrong Liberal Judaism was in taking this stand. With the exception of a small orthodox group the vast majority of Zionists have no belief in a Messiah, even though they have been busy promoting the national restoration of the Jewish people.

A second factor which impelled Liberal Judaism to give up belief in a Messiah was its desire to be in a better position to deal with the Christian challenge. Joseph Albo, a learned Spanish Jew (1380-1444), composed a work which he named *Ikarim* (Principles) in which he attempted to formulate the principles of Jewish belief. One of his chief objects was to prove to the Jewish people that theirs was the true religion while Christianity was a false religion. It is said that he felt that belief or nonbelief in a Messiah has no effect on the Jew's religious status. In fact, he is said, by implication at least, to have recommended that Jews give up belief in a Messiah, hoping thereby to cut the ground from underneath Christianity, where the person of the Messiah is at the heart of its faith. Liberal

Judaism of the nineteenth century adopted this line of reasoning.[39]

A third factor which had much to do with the discarding of the belief in a Messiah by Liberal Judaism was related to the general state of things in Europe of the nineteenth century. The great strides made in science, industry, education, and in the direction of attainment of democratic goals generated an atmosphere of optimism concerning human destiny. Man was believed to be essentially good. He was expected to receive from science all the power he needs; from education, all the knowledge he must have; from democracy, all the freedom he wants. The millennium was seen to be approaching, but it was a millennium which was indifferent to the actual spiritual state of man, a millennium without God.

It was tragic that German Jewry, the fountainhead of Liberal Judaism, should have seen in the prevailing state of affairs with its materialistic mood the fulfillment of Israel's mission of the messianic hope of the prophets of the Old Testament. The effect which that era had on the German Jews may be seen from the following excerpts from addresses made at a rabbinical conference, held at Frankfort-on-the-Main, Germany, in July, 1845.

One rabbi declared that "everywhere the Jewish doctrine of the Messiah is fulfilling itself rapidly. Everywhere the emancipation of mankind is being striven for so that a morally pure and holy life may be possible of being lived by man on this earth."[40]

Another rabbi said that the conference "should state that

[39]Steven S. Schwarzschild, "The Personal Messiah—Towards The Restoration of a Discarded Doctrine," *Judaism* (New York), Spring, 1956.

[40]David Philipson, *The Reform Movement in Judaism* (New York: The Macmillan Co., 1931), p. 176.

we are now entering upon a period of redemption. Freedom and virtue are spreading, the world is growing better."[41]

Still another rabbi held that "in our days . . . the ideals of justice and the brotherhood of men have been so strengthened through the laws and institutions of modern states, that they can never again be shattered; we are witnessing an ever nearer approach of the establishment of the Kingdom of God on earth through the strivings of mankind."[42]

About a century following the Frankfort conference German Jewry disappeared under the Nazi regime. Many of the German Jews who survived made their way to Palestine, there to help with the task of rebuilding the Jewish national homeland and thus fulfill the centuries-old Jewish hope which the grandfathers of these German refugees repudiated at the Frankfort conference.

One of the rabbis at the Frankfort conference, who tried unsuccessfully to stop the trend towards the elimination of the prayers for the coming of the Messiah, reminded his listeners that "all great events in the world's history have been accomplished by great personalities; may we not then confidently expect that this greatest and highest consummation of all, the ushering in of religious harmony, peace and brotherhood will be accomplished through one sent of God?"[43] This rabbi was certainly on Biblical ground, for the Old Testament knows of no messianic age without a messianic person, and no messianic program which leaves the human heart unregenerated.

[41]*Ibid*, p. 178.
[42]*Ibid*.
[43]*Ibid.*, p. 179.

VI. CONCLUDING OBSERVATIONS ON THE CAUSE OF THE JEWISH SPIRITUAL DILEMMA

The present religious crisis began in the nineteenth century. It came in the wake of the political emancipation of the Jewish communities in the countries of Western Europe. It is the nineteenth-century phase of the religious crisis which was precipitated when the destruction of the Temple in the year 70 caused the cessation of the sacrificial cult.

To appreciate the causal relationship between the termination of the sacrificial cult and the religious crisis one needs only to read the numerous detailed laws and instructions regarding the sacrificial worship as recorded in the Pentateuch. A continual offering was to be sacrificed in the Temple every day in the year, consisting of two lambs, one in the morning and one in the evening. Additional sacrifices were to be offered on the Sabbath day, on the first day of the month, and on the appointed festivals.[44]

> It shall be a continual burnt-offering throughout your generations . . .
>
> Exodus 29:42

When rabbinism realized that it might take a long time before the sacrificial worship would be restored, it reconstructed Judaism from a religion with sacrifices to a religion without sacrifices. Prayers were composed into which were incorporated certain portions from the Pentateuch dealing with the institution of the sacrifices. These were to be recited with the added petition that God would accept these recited prayers in place of the sacrifices.

[44]See Exodus 29:38-42; Leviticus 23; Numbers 28 and 29.

But this was to be an interim measure, a stopgap as it were. The Prayer Book is replete with passages in which the Synagogue bemoans the cessation of the sacrificial worship, as seen from the following passage from the Musaph and Minchah prayers for the Day of Atonement.

> But we are sinners and trespassers.
> Wherewith shall our heavy iniquities be atoned for?
> The glory of the Temple has been removed from us,
> Since then there is no forgiveness or atonement for us.
> The burnt-offerings and sacrifices ceased,
> How shall we confront Him who dwells in the heavenlies?
>
> *   *   *   *   *   *
>
> If there is no atonement, whence shall help come for those tainted daily in sin, iniquity, and wickedness?

Accordingly, we find in the Prayer Book many heart-touching petitions for the speedy restoration of the sacrificial worship, as seen from the following excerpt:

> May it please Thee, Jehovah our God, and the God of our fathers, King of mercy, to have abundant compassion upon us and upon Thy Sanctuary, and rebuild it speedily, and increase its glory . . . And lead us to Zion, Thy city, with singing, and with an everlasting joy to Jerusalem, the place of Thy Sanctuary; and there we shall offer before Thee the sacrifices enjoined on us, the continual sacrifices according to their order, and the additional sacrifices according to their ordinance.

The Mishnah devotes one of its main six divisions to a detailed description of the rules and regulations which govern the Temple sacrifices. The pious Jews have for centuries studied and meditated over these Talmudic chapters, as if the Temple had never been destroyed.

When Palestine was devastated by Rome and the Jews dispersed, the Jewish people lost all knowledge of their genealogy. But there is one group of Jews who to this day have retained their genealogical connections with the past. These are the Jews who are descendants of the family of Aaron the high priest. The reason for this is twofold: First, these Aaronic Jews are duty-bound to pronounce the Aaronic benediction in the synagogue on the regular festivals. Second, they are the means of preserving the priesthood for the day when the Temple cult will be reestablished.

If the State of Israel were to regain the Temple site, now in the hands of the tiny Arab state of Jordan, would the Jews rebuild the Temple and restore the sacrifices? The answer that is possible to give now is that the Temple would probably be rebuilt, but it is highly doubtful whether world Jewry would favor the reinstitution at this time of the sacrificial worship. And yet the fact remains that if the Old Testament revelation is God's last word to man, then there is no other way whereby a Jew who rejects the New Testament revelation can approach God except by way of the Old Testament sacrifices. This is the essence of the Jewish religious dilemma. The two horns of this dilemma are the rejection of Jesus Christ and the cessation of the sacrificial worship of the Old Testament. In its persistent efforts to get away from Jesus, Judaism was forced to move further and further away from the Old Testament. In the process of this movement away from the Bible many Jews lost faith in God's Word, faith in a Messiah, faith in a hereafter and, finally, faith in God. This is the source of the spiritual conflict in the Jewish soul.

Part Three

PREPARING THE WAY FOR
ISRAEL'S REDEMPTION

CHAPTER 8

THE REMNANT OF ISRAEL

AT THE PRESENT JUNCTURE of Jewish history there are three agencies which under God may be used to bring about the spiritual rebirth of the Jewish people. They are: The Remnant of Israel, the State of Israel, and the Christian Church.

The Sinai Covenant was a covenant between two parties. One of the two parties is God, the initiator of the covenant; the other party is Israel. On the divine side, the covenant with Israel was to last indefinitely, as long as there will be an Israel. We have in the Old Testament the promise that God will renew the covenant, that He will replace it with a better and more perfect one, but He would never abrogate it.[1] On Israel's side, it was anticipated that from time to time she would break the covenant by merely failing to live up to its requirements. With this in mind, sacrifices were instituted whose purpose was to maintain the covenant and to repair it whenever broken. But Israel entered the covenant freely. She had the liberty to accept it, and the liberty to decline. But once she accepted it, she can never as a nation abrogate it. She can break it, and she has done this many times in the past. But as a nation she can never abrogate the covenant.

In what position with relation to the covenant is the individual Israelite? The Sinai Covenant made with the whole nation of Israel is valid for every born Israelite in

[1]Genesis 17:7; Jeremiah 31:31-34 (31:30-33 Heb.); 31:35-37 (31: 34-36 Heb.).

the sense that it affords him the opportunity to confirm the covenant for himself, or not to confirm it. As the nation standing at Sinai had to choose to accept or not to accept, so every born Israelite has to make the same decision for himself personally. The Bar Mitzvah[2] is the externalization or the formalization of the decision of the born Israelite to accept the covenant. But the acceptance of the covenant is an inward and spiritual experience and may take place before the Bar Mitzvah, after it, or without it. The faith of the Jew is most certainly a "religious faith freely chosen."[3] Actually, it is this inward, willing, and joyful surender to God and this dedication of oneself to the ideals and goals of the covenant which in the sight of God is true acceptance of the covenant. If the individual Israelite sins against the covenant faith he, like the nation of Israel, is disciplined, but he remains in the covenant. The difference between the nation of Israel and the individual Israelite in relation to the covenant is this: the nation of Israel is in the covenant, whether it likes it or not. The covenant with the nation of Israel is an indissoluble union. The individual Israelite is not in the covenant unless and until he freely accepts the covenant for himself, and he can refuse to accept it. If he refuses to accept the covenant he is "cut off" from Israel. When Israel was a theocracy, to be "cut off" from Israel meant at times to be put to death. However, basically to "be cut off" from Israel suggests to be placed outside the Israel Covenant.

This setting aside of those who are merely of the seed of Abraham in the flesh has been going on throughout Jewish history. It began in the days of Abraham. Ishmael, though of the seed of Abraham, was placed outside of the

[2]Confirmation ceremony of a Jewish boy at the age of thirteen.
[3]Lionel Rubinoff, in *Judaism* (New York), Fall, 1961.

covenant. Esau, who like Jacob was a son of Isaac and Rebecca, was removed from the covenant because he "despised his birthright" (Genesis 25:34). With the exception of a few individuals, all those who left Egypt at the age of twenty or older were "cut off" from Israel in the wilderness. The vast majority of the people of the northern kingdom of Israel and many of the southern kingdom of Judah were rejected from Israel's covenant.

In every age and generation there is a remnant which is faithful to the covenant. It is called in the Bible the remnant of Israel. Such a remnant is alive in America today.

> When I look at the American Jewish scene, I find much that is heartening. We are witnessing the maturing of a generation . . . deeply faithful to the Covenant whose level of Jewish literacy would have been inconceivable thirty years ago. An example of this is the coming into being of YAVNEH, a national organization of religious Jewish students with chapters at leading campuses across the nation. This has been an entirely spontaneous development; while professional Jewish organizations pour millions and millions of dollars into activities kept alive artificially and with the greatest of effort, YAVNEH came into being by itself when Orthodox students at various universities were drawn together by the need to pray, to observe Kashruth[4] and have regular sessions of Torah study. Before any one realized what was going on, a national organization came into being, financed by members' dues . . . At the second annual convention, held during the past Labor Day weekend, close to 400 students attended . . .

> There is no doubt in my mind that American Jewry is living through a period of decision. Those segments

[4]Kashruth—Observance of dietary laws.

of the community whose interest is primarily a secular one, will, within a relatively few generations lose their interest in any form of Jewish life and thereby make unnecessary the diverse "reinterpretations" so prevalent today. To those who remain, the Covenant and its obligations will remain.[5]

There is also a remnant in the State of Israel.

The election of Isarel and the Covenant gave us rights, but also imposed upon us heavy duties and we were punished when we did not carry them out. 'Because of our sins we were exiled from our land.' On the other hand it is the Covenant that stood us in good stead, and spared us from annihilation among the nations so that, in Isaiah's words, 'a remnant will return.' More than this, part of the remnant has returned in our own generation.[6]

We demanded from the peoples of the world the chance to renew our State. We based this demand upon events in the past and we won. Now we must really and truly build the present upon the foundations of the past and fill with true Jewish content the modern political framework that we have gained. Generation after generation received the spark of tradition and treasured it lest it become extinguished. Zion and Jerusalem were never allowed to escape our memories. They were enshrined in our festivals and in our prayers . . . Tradition did not remain a dead weight, but for thousands of years it was a living possession. This tradition reminded us daily of our national history and of our mission. Now that we have been allowed to resume our history in our land and State, it is incumbent upon us to fulfill our task.[7]

[5]Michael Wyschogrod, in *Judaism* (New York), Fall, 1961.
[6]Aron Barth, *The Modern Jew Faces Eternal Problems* (Jerusalem: The Religious Section Of The Youth And Hechalutz Department Of the Zionist Organization, 1956), p. 78; used by permission.
[7]*Ibid.*, p. 87.

This perennial weeding-out process, so conspicuous in Jewish history, by which individuals and whole groups become separated from the nation, has as its chief purpose the spiritual cleansing of the nation in preparation for its divinely appointed mission. At the risk of repetition, let us review again that revealing passage in Exodus in which the nation Israel was informed for the first time that God has a mission for it to discharge.

> You have seen what I did to the Egyptians, and how I bare you on eagles' wings, and brought you unto myself. Now therefore, if you will obey my voice indeed, and keep my covenant, then you shall be mine own possession from among all peoples; for all the earth is mine: And ye shall be unto me a kingdom of priests, and a holy nation.
>
> Exodus 19:4-6, A.S.V.

As soon as Israel accepted the covenant in the wilderness, the process of purification began, designed to make of her a holy nation, and thus render her fit for her priestly mission to the nations of the earth. The accomplishment of this purifying process was one of the functions of the covenant, but it was not to be achieved without much suffering for Israel.

The end of Israel's spiritual cleansing is described in many parts of the prophetic writings of the Old Testament, of which the following passage is the best example:

> A remnant shall return, even the remnant of Jacob, unto the mighty God. For though thy people, Israel, be as the sand of the sea, only a remnant of them shall return . . .
>
> Isaiah 10:21-22

And it shall come to pass, that he that is left in Zion, and he that remaineth in Jerusalem, shall be called holy, even everyone that is written among the living in Jerusalem; when the Lord shall have washed away the filth of the daughters of Zion, and shall have purged the blood of Jerusalem from the midst thereof, by the spirit of justice, and by the spirit of burning.

Isaiah 4:3-4

Throughout Jewish history the remnant of Israel has lived in the midst of the nation. When Israel's cleansing will have reached its end, the remnant of Israel will become completely separated from nominal Israelites. From other prophetic writings in the Old Testament we know that Israel's sufferings before the end of her present history will constitute the hour of her greatest peril.[8] Every one that will come out alive from that hour of trial and tribulation will be holy. Since only the remnant will remain alive, the remnant alone will constitute the nation of Israel; and since every one of that remnant will be holy, all Israel will be holy. It is quite possible that this kind of Old Testament teaching became the basis of Paul's declaration that "all Israel shall be saved" (Romans 11: 26).

[8]Jeremiah 30:4-7; Zechariah 13:8-9.

CHAPTER 9

THE STATE OF ISRAEL

INTRODUCTION—THE STATE OF ISRAEL AND
THE RELIGIOUS PROBLEM

I. INTRODUCTION

THE OVERWHELMING MAJORITY of the participants in the
symposia conducted by *Commentary* and *Judaism* showed
a sympathetic interest in the State of Israel. In this they
reflect the sentiments of the vast majority of American
Jewry, indeed of world Jewry. But quite a few betrayed a
concern over the possibility that Israel may turn out to
be just another nation. They felt that for Israel to become
like other nations is contrary to the spirit and destiny of
the Jewish people. The disappointment over Israel's present position in the world has been expressed in the following statement: "The trouble with Israel is that it is such
a big idea in the perspective of world history and such a
little idea in the perspective of modern history."[1]

If by "world history" the writer had in mind the ancient
world, then we should remember that comparatively speaking the ancient world was a small world, as it consisted
chiefly of countries located in the Mediterranean region.
But as a matter of historical record, even in that small
world Israel was not a "big idea" politically as compared

[1] Elihu Katz, in *Commentary* (New York), April, 1961.

with such states as Egypt, Assyria, Babylon, Persia, Greece, and Rome. Israel's greatness in world history is due to the unique character of her spiritual heritage. And it is this spiritual heritage which was to give her a distinctive place among the nations of the earth.

> Behold, I have taught you statutes and judgments, even as Jehovah my God commanded me, that ye should do so in the land whither ye go to possess it. Keep therefore and do them; for this is your wisdom and your understanding in the sight of the nations, which shall hear all these statutes, and say, Surely this great nation is a wise and understanding people.
>
> Deuteronomy 4:5-6

II. THE STATE OF ISRAEL AND THE RELIGIOUS PROBLEM

For centuries the Jew has been told that when the Jewish people will regain their national homeland they will be able to comply fully with God's commandments, for only in the Land of Israel can the Jew truly fulfill the Torah. The reconstitution of the State of Israel exploded this notion. It is actually less possible for an Orthodox Jew to live religiously in the State of Israel than in many Gentile lands. With the five-day working week in practice in America it is entirely possible for the Orthodox Jew living in America to observe the Sabbath. If his occupation should require his presence on the Sabbath day, he can either be relieved by a Gentile employee or he could switch to another job. Even in the armed forces Jewish service men are usually relieved of their duties during the high holidays. Not so in Israel, where Jews must attend to all vital and necessary functions at all times. During his visit in America an Orthodox Jewish leader from the State of Israel tried to persuade the student body of a Yeshiva[2] school in the New York area to move to Israel. But his arguments were of no avail, for both the students and their teachers doubted that they could live as Jewishly in the State of Israel as they can in America.[3] If a pipe were to burst in their school in Israel on the Sabbath day, Jewish plumbers would have to repair it on the Sabbath day. If a fire were to start somewhere in their school, Jewish firemen would have to extinguish it even on the Sabbath day. If they were drafted into the Israel army, they would have to attend to their duties even on the Sabbath day. And so it is that in Israel the Jew is being reminded daily that Rabbinic Judaism and even some of the laws of Moses are incompatible with the life of a modern state.

The discussion which follows is based on material from several sources, including *Israel: The Sword and The Harp* (1969) by Ferdynand Zweig, *Israel Observed* (1981 repr.) by William Frankel, and especially *Perpetual Dilemma—Jewish Religion in the Jewish State* (1976) by S. Zalman Abramov (distributed by the World Union for Progressive Judaism). At the time of the writing of this well-documented and most informative work, Abramov was deputy speaker of the Knesset (Parliament) and had for some seventeen years been a member of the Committee on Law and Constitution. Between 1963 and 1972 he was the Knesset representative in the Council of Europe, and the Associate Editor of the Encyclopedia of Zionism and Israel.

1. The Electoral System in Israel

Elections for seats in the Knesset are held at least once every four years, or sooner if so ordered by the Knesset. Neither the

[2] A Rabbinic school with the emphasis on Talmudic studies.
[3] Moshe Zvi Neriah, "Judaism and Its Mission," article in *Forum for the Problems of Zionism, Jewry and the State of Israel* (Jerusalem, Israel), Vol. 4, Spring, 1959.

President nor the Prime Minister can dissolve the Knesset. In accordance with the Basic Law of the Knesset of 1958 members are elected by "general, national, direct, equal, secret and proportional elections." Unlike the British and American systems, which are based on geographic or regional constituencies, in Israel the people do not vote for individual candidates but for political party lists which are used nationwide. The higher in the list a candidate finds himself, the better chance he has of being elected if his party happens to win a sufficient number of votes. Thus the members of the Knesset do not owe their election directly to the voters, but to their political party.

A group of 750 eligible Israeli citizens can form a political party and submit a list to the voters. A new party must deposit a certain sum of money with the election authority, which is forfeited if the party fails to win a single seat in the Knesset. The Knesset has 120 seats, and to win a seat one needs at least 1 percent of the total votes cast in a particular election.

The electoral system in Israel makes possible a victory, in a sense, of the small parties over the larger ones, since it is much easier to pick up 1 percent of the total votes cast in any election than to win a majority of votes in any particular district. This system has resulted in a proliferation of political parties, making it difficult for any major party to win an absolute majority of the votes. For example, fifteen parties were represented in the second Knesset, ten in the third, and thirteen in the ninth; thirty-one parties presented lists to the voters for the tenth (1981) Knesset, and ten parties won seats. To form a single-party government, that party must win at least sixty-one seats in the Knesset. At no time since the formation of the state has any party won enough votes to form a single-party government. Thus every government in Israel since the beginning of the present state has been a coalition government.

The Labor Party had been the dominant party until 1977, yet every government it formed was a coalition government.

Since it could not or would not compromise with the ideological policies of other large parties, such as the General Zionists (liberal) or Herut, the Labor Party brought into the government the Religious Parties. The number of votes which the Religious Parties have gained over the years has varied between 12 and 15 percent, giving them between fifteen and eighteen seats in the Knesset. The National Religious Party (NRP) is the largest religious political party. Between 1949 and 1977 the NRP was a constant ally of the Labor government.

The price exacted by the NRP for its participation in the government was high. Since 1959 the NRP has held three of the most important cabinet posts in the government: the Ministry of Religious Affairs, the Ministry of the Interior, and the Ministry of Social Welfare. The Ministry of Religious Affairs "supervises holy places, supports theological seminaries, subsidizes the construction of synagogues, churches, mosques, and other denominational institutions and audits religious councils." Thus the NRP has exercised wide control over the administration of the religious affairs in the country and has an important voice in the matter of rabbinic appointments, granting of financial subsidies to Yeshivot (Talmudic schools), and the construction of synagogues, as well as appointments to the 186 local religious councils.

The post of Ministry of the Interior gives the NRP control of the finances of the municipal and local councils and control of the allocation of suitable financial support for the maintenance of the local religious councils. It is also in charge of administering the Population Registry Law, which enables it to determine that anyone registered as a Jew is indeed a Jew in accordance with the requirements of Talmudic law.

The post of Ministry of Social Welfare gives the NRP an opportunity to be in close contact with thousands of disadvantaged Israelis and thus influence their political allegiance.

The final religious authority is the Chief Rabbinical Council, presided over by the Ashkenazi and Sephardi Chief Rabbis. Its functions include the implementation of Kashrut (dietary laws), registration of marriages and divorces, the sanction of rabbinical ordination, and the rendering of judgments in matters of religious law. The Chief Rabbis preside over the Supreme Rabbinical Court, which hears appeals from decisions of District Rabbinical Courts. The local councils employ a rabbinical staff of four hundred rabbis.[4]

Aware that Talmudic Judaism has no guidelines for problems relating to foreign affairs, national defense, and the economy of a modern state (since Talmudic Judaism evolved in the centuries during which the Jewish people had no political independence), the NRP is perfectly satisfied to leave these areas to the "secularists"—by which term is meant non-observant Jews—as long as the NPR is given opportunity to deal with the Jew's personal life and family affairs. Its ultimate aim is to transform the State of Israel into a Talmudic state. This it hopes to accomplish in two ways: through a large network of religious schools where the study of the Talmud occupies a prominent, and even a central, place; and through the enactment of "religious laws" dealing with such matters as dietary laws, the observance of the weekly Sabbath, national holidays, and marriage and divorce.

When NRP members are reminded that the Declaration of Independence guarantees freedom of religion and conscience, they declare that the law of Moses and Israel (i.e., the Talmud) is binding on all Jews and takes precedence over any principles of Israeli democracy. "No one is at liberty to divest himself of it, even if he so desires. We are commanded to coerce. This is the pure truth according to the Torah."[5] However, this view is rejected by Dr. Rosenblueth, a prominent Orthodox educator,

---

[4]Israel Information Center, P.O.B. 13010, Jerusalem.
[5]*Hadat veHamedinah*, ed. Matetyahu (Mafdel, Jerusalem, 1964), p. 149.

who reminds us that the Sinai Covenant and Mosaic Law were accepted by the people of Israel out of their own free will.[6]

2. Marriage and Divorce Laws

In accordance with the Rabbinical Court Jurisdiction Law of 1953, marriage and divorce of Jews in Israel, whether nationals or alien residents, are under the exclusive jurisdiction of rabbinical courts. Marriage and divorce in Israel are to be performed in accordance with Jewish religious law. What is meant by "in accordance with Jewish religious law" was not specified. But the Orthodox interpreted it to mean "in accordance with Talmudic law," since the official rabbinate is made up of Orthodox Rabbis only. When this bill was presented to the Knesset, the Knesset was informed by the Orthodox Deputy Minister for Religious Affairs that to permit civil marriage and divorce would destroy the unity of the Jewish people; thus the laws of marriage and divorce must be taken as they are, "since it is impossible for the Knesset to amend or alter them."[7]

Speaking for the United Worker's Party, Eliezer Peri declared that this bill was conceived by the religious politicians, who drew only 12 percent of the vote in the election, and it was being imposed on the nation because the coalition government needed to keep the religious members in the cabinet. Turning to the Orthodox representatives, he said:

If you really wish to inculcate faith in, and respect for, religion, your present methods will yield the opposite result. Will you, by a coercion, lead to faith? True faith and coercion are mutually exclusive. You are only arousing indignation against yourselves; each single non-believer can tell you how indignant

[6]*HaAretz* (Tel Aviv), September 25, 1965.
[7]*Knesset Record* (Jerusalem), 14:1477.

and humiliated he is when he presents himself to the rabbi at
his wedding. If you coerce us to submit to this authority [of the
officiating Rabbi], you are not cultivating faith but hypocrisy; . . .
You are humiliating religion itself.[8]

Isaiah Leibowitz, professor at the Hebrew University and an
outstanding Orthodox Jew, said that

> the contention that the recognition by the state of civil mar-
> riage will split the Jews is false. . . . One who raises this argu-
> ment is ignoring the reality of hundreds of thousands of Jews
> in the Western world who lead Torah-truc lives under laws which
> provide for civil marriage and divorce. . . . We must not, how-
> ever, expect the rabbinic authorities to consider the matter ob-
> jectively, for they have a vested interest in it.[9]

"From a religious point of view," he said,

> there can be no greater abomination than a secular state which
> recognizes religious institutions as state institutions, maintains
> them, and imposes on the general public, not religion, but cer-
> tain religious functions by an arbitrary selection determined by
> party politics, and all this while claiming that this is not a Hal-
> achic State [a state ruled by Talmudic law], but one where civil
> law prevails. And what about a rabbinate whose appointment,
> jurisdiction, and salary are determined by the secular authority,
> whose status is thus comparable to that of the police force, the
> sanitary department, the post office. There can be no greater
> humiliation for a religion, nothing that detracts so much from
> its influence, than the establishment and maintenance of reli-
> gious institutions by a secular state. . . . All this is a falsification
> of social and religious truth, and a source of spiritual and in-
> tellectual corruption.[10]

[8]*Knesset Record* (Jerusalem), 16:1472.
[9]Quoted in *Ovnaim* (Tel Aviv), Spring 1966, p. 62.
[10]*Beterem* (Jerusalem), September 10, 1959.

3. The Talmudic Schools

While the Ministry for Religious Affairs, the Chief Rabbinate, and the local religious councils make up the political-religious establishment in Israel, Orthodoxy is molded by the Chief Rabbinate and the heads of Yeshivot (the Talmudic schools). Of these the strongest influence on the Rabbis is exerted by the Yeshivot Gdolot, institutions for higher Torah studies. They enroll young men from seventeen to twenty-five years old. The entire time of study is dedicated to the Talmud, none to the Bible or secular subjects. Even the study of the Hebrew language and literature and Jewish history is excluded. No studies of relevance to contemporary life are offered. It is from these Yeshivot that the majority of rabbis and Dayanim (rabbinical arbitrators) hail, and it is these Yeshivot that are the source of the intellectual climate of the rabbinate.[11]

This Yeshiva world, a leading educator declares,

> breeds an air of self-assurance and of arrogance which all leads to extremism and fanaticism. Alienation from the secular state has turned into hostility towards the state; these feelings of hostility find their expression in repeated acts of violence: throwing stones and breaking windows of cars driven on the Sabbath, injuring doctors and nurses driven in those cars, attacking the police who seek to protect the attacked, organizing attacks on Christian mission schools . . . all these alarming symptoms which testify to the methods adopted by the militant Orthodox to bring the Kingdom of Heaven nearer. These are the products of hatred and self-isolation.[12]

It is this Yeshiva environment that determines the quality of religious life in Israel. Very few of these Yeshiva-trained Rabbis

---

[11]S. Zalman Abramov, *Perpetual Dilemma: Jewish Religion in the Jewish State* (Cranbury, N.J.: Associated University Presses, Inc. [P.O.B. 421, 08512], 1976), p. 239.

[12]*Temurot* (Tel Aviv), April 1964.

have a formal university or even a secondary-school education. Hardly any of them have a knowledge of Western culture, of any European language, or of contemporary thought. Though employed and paid by the state, many have little knowledge of the social and moral problems of those they are appointed to serve.[13]

4. Who Is a Jew?

The affairs of the Upper Nazareth community were administered by a coalition of the local Labor Party and the local NRP. It was an uneasy alliance and a certain Rina Eitani, an official of the local Labor Party, incurred the displeasure of the NRP. A neighbor informed the official in charge of the local Population Registry that Mrs. Eitani's mother was Gentile. An inquiry was initiated in the Records Office in Germany where Rina Eitani came from and it was revealed that her mother, a Gentile, had married a Jew. Upon the receipt of this information the registration official requested Rina to surrender her passport, which she supposedly had obtained by misrepresentation. To forestall an unpleasant situation, the Ministry of the Interior advised Rina that she could obtain Israeli citizenship by naturalization—i.e., as a Gentile. A Jewish person immigrating to Israel becomes a citizen upon arrival. To make things worse, the local NRP leaders intimated that more such cases would be disclosed.

The Eitani affair created a furor, especially when all the details of her case came to light. During the Nazi period her mother, though an Aryan, stuck to her Jewish husband and her children, even though this entailed much suffering for her at the hands of the Nazis. Rina, being half Jewish, was also exposed to persecution. She managed to survive, and when

[13]S. Zalman Abramov, Op. Cit., p. 241.

the Nazis were defeated, she made her way to Palestine in defiance of the British ban on immigration. During the War of Independence she served in the Israel Defense Army. She subsequently was married and became active in the municipal affairs in Upper Nazareth, where she was elected to the town council.

The Israel Supreme Court declared the action of the Upper Nazareth registration offical contrary to the law. It explained that the Law of Return, which deals with immigration, is a secular law; thus the term *Jew* for the purpose of this law should be interpreted in its commonly accepted meaning rather than in accordance with Talmudic law, which defines a Jew as one who is born of a Jewish mother or is converted to the Jewish faith. For the purpose of the Law of Return Mrs. Eitani was Jewish. Commenting on this case Jacob Talmon, professor at the Hebrew University, said that "if the non-Jewish blood of the mother was indeed an insuperable barrier, surely there was here a case of biological racialism overriding spiritual content and freedom of choice. And the panacea of religious conversion, even if granted by rabbis, smacked too much of coercive pressure."[14]

On February 9, 1970, an amendment to the Population Registry Law of 1965 was presented to the Knesset for action. The amendment stated that for the purpose of this law the term *Jew* refers to a person born of a Jewish mother or one who is converted to Judaism and is not a member of another religion. The Orthodox insisted that the words "converted to Judaism" be followed by the words "in accordance with the Halakhah," i.e., Talmudic laws. They were thus aiming to nullify conversions performed by Conservative and Reform Rabbis who did not follow all the details of Talmudic law pertaining to conversion of Gentiles to Judaism. Golda Meir, who was then

Prime Minister of the Labor government, refused to yield on this point.

During the debate in the Knesset one of the leaders of the Mapam (United Workers Party) read a letter addressed to Golda Meir, written by a member of Kibbutz Revadim, a young man from Holland. His mother was Gentile, his father Jewish. During the Nazi occupation of Holland he was made to wear the yellow badge and experienced many disabilities on account of his Jewish identity. After the war he came to Israel and served in the Israeli army, where he lost both legs. In his letter he asked three questions:

> (a) What should the offspring of a mixed marriage in Europe do, where it is the father who is the Jew? In Europe we are regarded as Jews, and here we are considered non-Jews. (b) Do you think I was right in coming here? Do you think that there is a place for me here as a "non-Jew"? (c) Was I right in doing what other Jews do, that is, to join the army? Did I lose my legs fighting for a country that is truly my homeland? Regarding myself as a Jew, I arrived here as an Oleh [an immigrant] and served in the army. Evidently this was not enough. What shall I, as a Jew, do? Shall I remain here and feel ashamed because my mother was not Jewish, or shall I return to Holland and feel ashamed because my father is a Jew?"[15]

To the question, Why could not this young man solve his problem by conversion to Judaism? the answer is that he believed that because his father is Jewish and because he had immigrated to Israel and served in the Israeli army he had already proved his total commitment and real conversion to Judaism. As a secularist, he did not believe he needed to do anything else to prove his dedication to the Jewish faith.

The amendment was passed. It declares that for the purpose of registration the term *Jew* identifies a person born of a Jewish mother or one who is converted to Judaism. But the words

[15]*Knesset Record* (Jerusalem), 56:739.

"in accordance with Halakhah" following "converted to Judaism" were not included in the bill. The labor government worked for the passage of this bill in order not to precipitate a government crisis. But many in the Knesset voted against the amendment.

5. Orthodox Opposition to Non-Orthodox Congregations

Since the laws of the State of Israel guarantee freedom of religion, Conservative and Reform groups are free to establish synagogues in Israel. But the Orthodox have been seeking to prevent non-Orthodox groups from opening up places of worship. The following three episodes are culled from a larger number of instances.

In 1962 Sharon Progressive (a term used to identify a non-Orthodox congregation) Congregation in Kfar Shmaryahu rented a hall in a local hotel for holding the upcoming High Holiday services. Shortly before Rosh Hashanah, the hotel manager informed the congregation that he had to cancel the arrangement as he was threatened by the local religious council with the withdrawl of the Kashrut certificate. This would have caused him considerable loss of business since observant Israeli Jews would not patronize his hotel. He therefore had no alternative but to cancel permission for the Reform congregation to hold their High Holiday services on his premises.

The congregation applied to the mayor of Kfar Shmaryahu for the lease of the Maccabi Sport Gymnasium, which was owned by the municipal council, and the services were held in the gymnasium. Under pressure from the local rabbinate, however, the mayor refused permission for this congregation to hold the Sukkot (Feast of Tabernacles) services. The congregation had to appeal to the High Court of Justice, which forced the mayor to grant permission. The press reported that when the judge asked the attorney for the municipal council whether it would be better for the congregation not to pray at all, he replied that it would have been better for them not to pray at all rather than to pray in the Reform manner.[16]

On May 25, 1967, the Rabbi of the Tel Aviv Progressive Congregation inquired of the Ministry of Religious Affairs whether it would be possible to acquire a burial plot for an American Jewish couple that requested in their will to be buried in accordance with the Reform ritual. The answer was given that no burial service could be held in accordance with the ritual of Progressive Judaism.[17]

The World Union for Progressive Judaism decided to hold its fifteenth international conference in 1968 in Jerusalem. The government sought to be helpful in many ways, and the Hebrew University placed its halls at the disposal of the conference. Some five hundred delegates from many countries, including some two hundred leaders of Reform Judaism from America, came to the conference, which began on July 3, 1968.

Prime Minister Levi Eshkol brought to the conference the greetings of the Israeli government. He spoke warmly to the convention and addressed it as "a Jew talking to fellow-Jews." "The very fact of holding this Conference in our holy and united capital . . . spells out triumph for the Jewish national trend in your movement." Appealing for a larger immigration of Reform Jews to Israel and realizing that such an appeal must carry the assurance that the Reform Synagogue would be recognized in Israel as a legitimate form of religious Judaism, Eshkol said: "I know that you hold views concerning religious life in this country. This, however, is not the occasion to deal with the matter. One thing is certain nevertheless; the

[16]*HaAretz* (Tel Aviv), October 10, 1962.
[17]Archive of Rabbi Moshe Zemmer (Tel Aviv).

life-style here will be molded by those who live here, and your influence will increase in proportion to the number of your adherents here."[18]

The program for the conference had scheduled a religious service at the Western Wall. Following the liberation of Old Jerusalem in the wake of the 1967 war, the Western Wall in Old Jerusalem became the point of attraction for pilgrims from far and near. In addition, regular services were instituted there three times daily. The organizers of the conference had made a formal application to hold a service for the delegates. The Ministry of Religious Affairs informed the representatives of the conference that the regulations of the Chief Rabbinate do not permit services where men and women worship together, since the section directly in front of the Western Wall is considered a synagogue.

The refusal to grant permission caused a public uproar in the whole country. The Orthodox denounced the Reform Synagogue as the betrayer of Judaism; some of them urged that the Reform Rabbis be driven out of the country, "for they seek to uproot the people, not only from its Torah, but also from its Land."[19] The Agudat Israel (an ultra-orthodox party) warned that the conflict with the Reform leaders "would be fought out as a war of survival."[20] The Knesset and the Cabinet were caught in a painful quandary. July 4, 1968, the day scheduled for the holding of the service, threatened to become a day of battle. Thousands of Yeshiva students and adherents of the Neturei Karta were directed to the Western Wall and instructed to use force, if necessary, in order to prevent the representatives of the conference from holding a service at the Western Wall.

[18]*Maariv*, July 4, 1968.
[19]*HaModia* (Jerusalem), June 14, 1968.
[20]S. Zalman Abramov, Op. Cit., p. 372.

The conference leaders decided not to hold the service at the Western Wall. Rabbi Maurice Eisendrath, president of the Union of American Hebrew Congregations, made this statement: "We have not been intimidated by threats of stone-throwing or bloodshed. Our decision not to hold an afternoon prayer service at the Western Wall was determined solely by the fear of physical violence to others, and, even more, of the possibility of political repercussions reflecting on Israel's rights in the Holy Places."[21] The *Jerusalem Post* made the following statement, which reflected the attitude of many of the Israeli Jews:

> The Reform group, by definition liberal and tolerant, found itself at a hopeless disadvantage in this struggle for its rights to pray as it wishes, against a section of the community that glories in its illiberalism, intolerance and fanaticism. They could not solemnly march out to battle, and capture the Wall. . . . But still we have reason to be grateful for their good sense in withdrawing in time from a painful conflict, and saving Jerusalem the likelihood of shame and disgrace. They showed more respect and regard for the Wall than many others have done.[22]

Has this deplorable religious condition changed since 1968? Not according to those who are well acquainted with religious life in Israel. Dov Rappel, a leading member of a religious kibbutz, states that

> many people in the Traditional congregations are searching for the truly traditional faith. . . . Unfortunately, however, most Orthodox rabbis in Israel have no common language with these people. . . . Immigrants from Western countries who wish to strengthen their Jewish identity expect their rabbis to have a broad Jewish education and a Jewish-religious approach to the problems of modern Man. . . . They very soon discover that the

[21]*The Jerusalem Post*, July 5, 1968.
[22]*Ibid*., July 7, 1968.

average Orthodox rabbi is not only unable to answer questions about the Hebrew language and Jewish history, but does not even know about such purely "religious" matters as Bible, religious philosophy, the meaning of the prayers and Kabbala [Jewish mystical teachings].[23]

At the twenty-second International Conference of the Reform synagogue, held in Jerusalem in 1983, Rabbi Richard Hirsch, Director General of the World Council for Progressive Judaism, told the delegates that "there are some religious Jews who, professing love of the Holy Land and obedience to God, fan the flames of religious fanaticism, violate the civil liberties of minority groups, advocate rule by force and prevent the evolution of conditions leading toward compromise." Continuing, this American-born Rabbi, who settled in Israel ten years ago, said: "We call their version of Judaism a perversion. Their love is blind, their Messianism false, and the zealotry dangerous. Their deeds defame the holy faith, desecrate the Holy One, and defile the Holy Land."[24]

To the Samaritan woman who asked Him which was the proper place for worship, at the Jerusalem Temple or at the site of the ruins of the Samaritan Temple, Jesus answered: "Woman, believe me, the hour is coming when neither on this mountain [Mount Gerizim, site of the Samaritan Temple destroyed by John Hyrcanus in 128 B.C.] nor in Jerusalem will you worship the Father. You worship what you do not know; we worship what we know, for salvation is from the Jews. But the hour is coming, and now is, when the true worshipers will worship the Father in spirit and truth, for such the Father seeks to worship him. God is spirit, and those who worship him must worship in spirit and truth" (John 4:21-24). About forty years later the Jerusalem Temple was destroyed.

[23]Dov Rappel, *Jerusalem Post*, International Edition, February 7, 1978.
[24]*The Jewish Post and Opinion* (Indianapolis), July 6, 1983.

CHAPTER 10

THE CHRISTIAN CHURCH

THE TENSION BETWEEN PARTICULARISM AND UNIVERSALISM IN ISRAEL'S FAITH—THE PROTESTANT REFORMATION—PRESENT-DAY JEWISH MESSIANISM—THE MESSIANIC ELEMENT IN THE COMMUNIST WORLD VIEW—THE PRECARIOUS INTERNATIONAL POSITION OF THE STATE OF ISRAEL—THE JEWISH PEOPLE CANNOT LIVE BY BREAD ALONE—THE HEBREW CHRISTIAN MISSION—A DAY OF OPPORTUNITY FOR THE CHRISTIAN CHURCH

I. THE TENSION BETWEEN PARTICULARISM AND UNIVERSALISM IN ISRAEL'S FAITH

THE MESSIANIC MOVEMENT of Jesus had a cosmopolitan orientation from its very inception. The "wise men from the east" who appeared in Jerusalem at the time of Christ's birth and the visit of the Greeks before His crucifixion symbolized the spiritual needs of the Gentile world. To meet that need was the commission which the disciples received from their risen Lord as recorded in these passages: "Go ye therefore, and make disciples of all the nations" (Matthew 28:19, A.S.V.) ; "Ye shall receive power, when the Holy Spirit is come upon you: and ye shall be my witnesses both in Jerusalem, and in all Judea, and Samaria, and unto the uttermost part of the earth" (Acts 1:8). It was this distinct cosmopolitan overtone in the message of the Gospel which became one of the important elements in Jewish opposition to the Gospel. The reason for it is inherent in the very nature of the Old Testament revelation.

In the days of Adam God dealt with one person. Whatever knowledge Adam possessed of God's redemptive plan must have become diluted in proportion as his descendants grew in numbers and lost contact with their ancestors. When, following the flood, God resumed His communication with man, He dealt with a family. When the descendants of Noah multiplied and spread out all over the then known world, in the course of time they grew into nations, far removed from their point of origin and from one another. The knowledge and worship of the true God with which they started out gradually became corrupt, so that when we reach the Abrahamic era we find that even Abraham's family had been infected with idolatry (Joshua 24:2).

The call of Abraham marked a new phase in the redemptive story of the Bible. It was a divine accommodation to the world's need. The emergence of nations brought into use the national approach. From now on a nation was to be used as the channel by which God's blessings were to be communicated to the nations of the earth. To ensure the effectiveness of this new divine approach, God created a new nation instead of merely choosing one of the existing nations. The call of Abraham, the circumstances surrounding the birth of Isaac, the life of Jacob, Joseph in Egypt, and the subsequent removal of Jacob and his household to Egypt where the Hebrews grew into a nation; their enslavement by the Egyptians and their deliverance under Moses; the passage through the Red Sea, the Sinai revelation, the forty years' wanderings in the wilderness, and the conquest of Canaan—all these and other historical events were, under God's overruling guidance, to engrave God's indelible stamp upon Israel's destiny in such a way that the very existence of Israel should testify of God's redemptive purpose for mankind. Under these circumstances God's purpose through Israel could be frustrated only if Israel were to perish, but God determined that Israel should not perish from the earth (Jer. 31:35-37 [31:34-36, Heb.]).

This divine consideration behind, as it were, the creation of Israel was unfolded in a remarkable passage in Genesis. The almost casual character of this revelation fills us with wonder, as it might have never been recorded, if not for the "incident" of the destruction of Sodom and Gomorrah.

> And Jehovah said, Shall I hide from Abraham that which I do [referring to the divine decree to destroy the wicked cities]; seeing that Abraham shall surely become a great and mighty nation, and all the nations of the earth shall be blessed in him? For I have known him, to the end that he may command his children and his household after him, that they may keep the way of Jehovah, to do righteousness and justice; to the end that Jehovah may bring upon Abraham that which he hath spoken of him.
>
> Genesis 18:17-19

Here we have several ideas of tremendous significance, all squeezed into a short passage. The aim and end of the call of Abraham is reiterated, that "all the nations of the earth shall be blessed in him." The realization of the divine purpose in the call of Abraham depended on the transmission by Abraham to his posterity of a knowledge of the divine purpose. In order to ensure the transmission of this knowledge, God took Abraham, as it were, into His confidence, "For I have known him, to the end that he may command his children and his household after him. . . ." The sight of the ruined cities of Sodom and Gomorrah was to serve as a constant warning to Abraham's descendants who shall dwell in that land that they must live in compliance with God's will, so that God's full purpose may be accomplished.

The Sinai Covenant with its laws and ordinances brought Jehovah and His people into such a close relationship that it was perfectly natural and human for Israel to come to look upon the God of Israel as primarily the God for Israel. This tendency to regard Jehovah as the God of Israel in this primarily national sense we call particularism; while the opposite tendency, which we meet especially in the prophetic writings and which considers Jehovah as the God of all nations and for all nations, we shall call universalism. At various periods of Jewish history there existed a tension between these two tendencies. By and large, in times of national distress Jewish particularism was strong. It was especially strong when Jewish Palestine was under the oppressive rule of pagan Rome in the first century of our era. It was therefore inevitable that when the messianic movement of Jesus emerged in the first century the universal character of its message should come into collision with the strong particularist or nationalist feeling prevailing among the Jewish people at that time.

And yet the state of the world in the first century of our era made emphasis of the international aspect of the Biblical message timely and urgent. Greek democracy had broken down. The Roman system of government moved in the direction of one-man rule with its attendant evils. Pagan religion was in disrepute. Pagan philosophy failed to provide a satisfactory solution to human problems or an adequate answer to life's ultimate questions.

At the same time a variety of events combined to foster a spirit of internationalism in the Mediterranean region. While the various nations lived within their national borders and retained their customs and way of life, world peace imposed by Roman power and Greek culture tended to blunt national exclusiveness and link the various peoples together. Men of various nationalities mingled with one another and came to see the universal aspect of human problems. Thus history—or rather God, the Lord of history—was preparing the Mediterranean world for a universal message of redemption. This is undoubtedly what Paul meant when he said that Jesus came into the world in the fullness of time (Galatians 4:4).

But history of those days has shown that Jewish particularism made it difficult for Israel as a nation to take full advantage of the opportunity to convey to the nations God's redemptive Word. The Jewish people of that day found it even difficult to effect a reconciliation with the Samaritans, who had lived in the center of Israel's land for about five or six centuries. This, in spite of the fact that the Pentateuch was the source of the Samaritan faith and the Samaritans were religiously so close to the Jews. Solomon's petition in his dedicatory prayer that the Temple might be a house of prayer for all nations was never fully granted. In the days of the second Temple the Gentiles were not permitted to approach Israel's God beyond the confines of the so-called court of the Gentiles; this was the outermost and lowermost Temple enclosure, which on the eve of the Passover became transformed into something like a marketplace, where oxen, sheep, and doves fit for sacrifices were sold and where the money changers had their tables, at which they were busy exchanging foreign currency into Temple coins.

It is true that sin-sick and spiritually hungry individual Gentiles were attracted to the synagogue, but if they resolved to become fully accepted into Israel's faith, they had to separate themselves from their relatives and from their people and become part of the Jewish nationality. This denationalizing effect attendant upon Gentile conversion to Israel's faith constituted a serious weakness in Israel's missionary activities. It is not the intention of God's redemptive purpose for the world to incorporate the nations of the earth into the Jewish nationality. Israel's mission is to bring the nations to God, not to make them members of the Jewish nation. We must differentiate between the central message of the Bible designed for all nations of the earth, and those features of Israel's Covenant faith which are important insofar as they serve to maintain the distinctive existence of Israel as the messianic people of God.

There was, however, another development which resulted in an undesirable overemphasis of the universal aspect of the Biblical faith. Even before ancient history reached its end, the center of gravity of world events began to shift from the Mediterranean region to the continent of Europe. That continent was inhabited by tribes and peoples in a semi-civilized or barbarous condition. They knew little or nothing of the civilization of Greece or Rome and probably less of the spiritual heritage of Israel.

With this shift of the center of gravity, the Christian Church was transplanted from the Mediterranean area of its origin to the European continent. This transfer of the Church from a highly intellectual area to a primitive environment, and the shrinking of Jewish influence in the

Church of the post-apostolic era, led to a gradual decline of Biblical knowledge within the Church. Under these circumstances it was inevitable that the Church should lose sight of Israel's unique position in the divine scheme of world redemption. At the same time, the deplorable state of the Jewish people in the Middle Ages, and the need to safeguard Jewish nationality in the Dispersion, led rabbinism to an overemphasis of Jewish particularism. And thus the gulf between Israel and the Church continued to widen.

II. THE PROTESTANT REFORMATION

The Protestant Reformation coincided in time with the great geographic discoveries which made the continent of America, the interior of Africa, and the Far East accessible to the peoples of Europe. These vast stretches of the earth with a non-Christian population exceeding by far the total population of Europe presented a great challenge to the Christian Church. In the nineteenth century the Protestant Church made a mighty effort to reach with the Gospel of Jesus the non-Christian peoples, many of whom by that time had come under the colonial rule of the white man. Christian activities in those countries were not confined to the purely religious sphere. Hospitals were opened up, schools and universities were founded, social welfare agencies were established, and the natives were taught a better way of life. These Christian activities indirectly paved the way for the present-day national independence movements of many of the submerged nations of Asia and Africa.

What caused this tremendous change from sullen hopelessness to grim resolve? A great many factors. The first were the teachings of Jesus, especially the Gospel of Luke and the companion Book of Acts. Here was good news for the poor, release to the captives, liberty to those who are oppressed, sight to the blind . . . blessed are you poor, blessed are you that hunger now, for you shall be satisfied; blessed are you that weep now, for you shall laugh. Woe to you that are rich, woe to you that are full now, for you shall hunger (Luke 6:20-25) . . . The words, compassionate deeds of Christ, and his death made him the friend of the poor, of sinners, of outcasts. It is very likely that the millions who zealously distributed the Bible never realized what new hope and what strong new determination the poor and oppressed derived from Jesus.[1]

The renewed interest in the Jewish people manifested by Protestant Christianity in the nineteenth century was part of its worldwide outreach. The tremendous increase of Biblical knowledge which followed in the wake of the Protestant Reformation opened the eyes of many Christians to Israel's unique place in God's redemptive plan. A feeling of grief and sorrow swept over many segments of the evangelical Church on account of the mistreatment which the Jews had for centuries experienced in Roman Catholic countries. Prayer circles sprang up where prayers were frequently made on behalf of Israel. Various societies were organized which sought to bring about an improvement in the economic, political and civil status of the Jews. Preoccupation with the Bible led many Christians to believe that the Jews were destined to reestablish themselves in Palestine.[2] Accordingly, many prominent Christians, espe-

[1]Frank C. Laubach, *Wake Up or Blow Up* (Westwood, N. J.: Fleming H. Revell Co., 1951), pp. 30-31.
[2]See S. A. Morrison, *Middle East Survey* (London: SCM Press Ltd. 1954), Chapter 2; Chaim Weizmann, *Trial and Error* (Philadelphia: Jewish Publication Society, 1949); Arthur W. Kac, *The Rebirth of the State of Israel* (London: Marshall, Morgan and Scott, 1960), Part One, Chapter 3.

cially in England and America, began—even before the rise
of the Zionist movement—an intensive political propaganda for the reconstitution of a Jewish State in Palestine.

At the same time intensive efforts were made to dis-
seminate among the Jews a knowledge of the New Testament. Appropriate literature was published through which
Christian people were seeking to point out how the gradual
unfolding in the Old Testament of the problems of sin, human suffering, redemption and holiness attained its fullness in the New Testament, and that Jesus Christ, to whom
the Old Testament was dear and precious, came indeed not
to destroy but to fulfill.

In the course of time this outpouring of Christian love
began to bear fruit in Jewish hearts and souls. It has been
estimated that in the nineteenth century alone some 200,-
000 Jews embraced the Christian faith. In certain Jewish
quarters sweeping statements have been made to the effect
that Jewish conversions are seldom genuine and that the
Jews who joined the Christian Church in the nineteenth
century did so to secure a "ticket of entry into European
society." There is no doubt that some Jewish conversions
were of that kind. In most cases the blame rests with
churches which admitted such into their fellowship. To
be sure, such churches were doing no worse than synagogues who admit into their membership people simply
because they were born Jews, even though they may be
atheists. It is no credit to the Jewish people to state that
Jewish conversions in the nineteenth century were for
ulterior motives, because those Jewish converts came from
the highest social layers of Jewish life. Most, and probably
all, were highly educated, and a good many belonged to
well-to-do Jewish families. Furthermore, in the nineteenth
century it was primarily in Germany where ulterior mo-

tives could tempt a Jew to affiliate with a Christian church. There have been many Jewish conversions in England, Holland, the Scandinavian countries, and America, where Jews have for many years enjoyed full citizenship status and where no ulterior motive existed.

That a great many Jewish conversions in the nineteenth century and since then have been genuine is clear to every unbiased person who will take the trouble to examine the facts.

> I am constantly amazed—states one Jewish observer— at the naiveté of our teachers and leaders who are surprised when I tell them that the best of our youth, our intellectuals, become Christians out of conviction . . . Our "leaders" do not believe it, to them a Jew never becomes a Christian unless he wants to better his position. That Christianity has drawn to itself such noble souls as Pascal, Novalis, Kirkegaard, Amiel, Dostoyevsky, Claudel, etc., etc., and that it exercises a most overwhelming influence on the most earnest truth-seekers among us, of that our teachers know nothing.[3]

Thousands of Jews all over the world belong to evangelical churches today for no other reason than that of a spiritual experience. At the beginning of the twentieth century some 250 churches in England and 125 churches in America were served by Hebrew Christian pastors. The evangelical Christian Church was spiritually enriched in the nineteenth century by the addition to its membership of Jews whose devotion to Jesus Christ knew no limit, and whose many and varied contributions to the Christian cause were of an enduring value. If we were to list only those converts of the nineteenth century whose Hebraic and Talmudic learning and many outstanding accomplish-

[3]Max Brod, quoted from *The Dawn* (Pittsburgh, Pa.), January-February, 1934.

ments single them out for honorable mention, their names would fill many pages of this study.[4]

The Jewish attitude to Hebrew Christians presents a tragic chapter in the annals of Jewish history. Jewish apologists usually attribute this attitude to the anti-Semitism of the medieval church. No account is taken of the fact that the same church persecuted, even more fiercely, Christians who dared to question her authority or charge her with having departed from the teachings of the New Testament. While it is true that the anti-Jewish spirit of the medieval Church influenced the Jewish attitude to Jewish converts to the Christian faith, this fact does not fully account for it. For Jewish antagonism to Hebrew Christians goes back to the first century, before Gentile Christianity became a dominating factor in world history. This is proven by certain rabbinic references, and especially by the so-called Birkat Ha-Minim prayer composed at the end of the first century for the purpose of forcing the Hebrew Christian to leave the synagogue.

The incontrovertible fact is that Jews, like millions of other people in the last nineteen centuries, have been drawn to Jesus Christ because they found in Him the answer to life's ultimate questions. What, however, proved decisive in their conversion was the conviction which they gained, when comparing the Old and New Testaments, that Jesus of the New Testament is the Messiah of the Old Testament. Of no little significance is this also, that many Jewish converts who prior to their conversion had been estranged from their people experienced as the result of their conversion a rekindling of their love for their people, and consequently reaffirmed their loyalty to the Jewish people.

[4]See, A. Bernstein, *Some Jewish Witnesses for Christ*, 1909.

III. PRESENT-DAY JEWISH MESSIANISM

In Part Two of this study we stated that in the years between the political emancipation of the Jews and the First World War, belief in a personal Messiah had largely been given up by the Jewish people. A messianic age to be achieved by education and material progress was substituted in the place of the messianic person. The destructive effects of the First World War, the rise of dictatorships, and the resurgence of human brutality following the First World War shattered this shallow nineteenth-century optimism, and the idea of a messianic age to be realized by purely human efforts was discredited.

The Nazi holocaust, with the destruction of more than a third of the Jewish nation, and the almost simultaneous rise of the State of Israel has caused a resuscitation of the messianic hope. This revival of Jewish messianism is linked to the following phenomena.

1. The Messianic Element in the Communist World View

In shaping his world view, Karl Marx borrowed certain leading ideas from the Bible and changed them in order to adapt them to his godless materialistic philosophy. According to this Communist philosophy, the goal to which the world is moving is not the Kingdom of God, but worldwide communism. The present world is the stage on which a conflict is waged between the forces of good as represented by communism and the forces of evil as represented by capitalism. In the final phase of this struggle, a day of judgment will come in which all the forces of capitalism will be crushed. The new world that will emerge will be a world in which all conflicts will cease. A new era of social harmony will be ushered in.

Much of the success of Communist propaganda in the non-Christian world, especially among the young people, is due to this world view of communism. Even the hungry have-not nations of Asia and Africa are stirred by questions of this nature. In this global conflict for men's minds, the secularized West is at a distinct disadvantage. Having given up, or divorced itself from, the Christian hope, the West has nothing to offer which is of ultimate significance. Christianity—not the West—is the real opponent of communism in this world struggle. This will explain the intensity of Communist hostility to Christianity. Indirectly, however, communism is turning men's thoughts back to the Bible, which is the source of messianism. And Biblical messianism, going back all the way to the opening chapters of Genesis, teaches that the world is moving to a goal, and this goal is the establishment of the kingdom of God on earth.

2. The Precarious International Position of the State of Israel

For the first time in over two thousand years Israel as a nation is being confronted with international tensions, and in the few years since she regained nationhood she has been involved in bitter international conflicts. Her most deadly enemies are the Arabs, who are closest to her by race and language. And behind the Arabs stands Communist Russia. Under these circumstances Israel is gaining the conviction that her salvation is inseparable from the salvation of the rest of mankind. Israel's present situation bears strong similarities to that period of her ancient history when she and the other smaller nations in the Near East were threatened in turn by the power of Assyria and Babylon. It was in the context of world events of that day that prophetic messianism was fully unfolded. Strikingly similar factors in the present state of the world are forcing Israel to return to the messianic hope of the Old Testament.

3. The Jewish People Cannot Live by Bread Alone

Lacking a vital faith in a personal God, many intellectual Jews turn to messianism both as a means by which to express their spiritual concerns and as the answer to the perplexing problems of our age.

THE FOLLOWING EXCERPTS REFLECT THE REVIVED JEWISH INTEREST IN MESSIANISM.

Jewish Dissatisfaction with the Status Quo

By Jewish tradition I mean the eternal sense of dissatisfaction with the status quo that motivated many Jews throughout the ages to use knowledge or the methods of science to solve empirical problems.[5]

Jewish Messianism Is a Guide to All Perplexed

If they [American Jews] still remain partly separate, it is less likely to be because of ghetto habits or fears; but it may also arise from the positive belief that, within the Jewish tradition of finding virtue here and soon, on earth, rather than in heaven, there is an important guide to all perplexed.[6]

Reaffirmation of Prophetic Ideals

Social and political history has been shaped, broadly, by two types of individuals: the prophets concerned with substance, and the priests concerned with form. The priests, watching over ritual and insisting that the so-

[5]Selwyn G. Geller, in *Judaism* (New York), Fall, 1961.
[6]Herbert Gold, in *Commentary* (New York), April, 1961.

called letter of the law be obeyed, have served the function of holding the group together. The prophet's role
has been a different one, and broader. He is the conscience of society, the poet of justice, the pragmatist of
hope. His acts disturb the immediate, reform the future,
and engender in people a non-ritualistic sense of their individual and group existence . . . but we can only fulfill
ourselves as men and as Jews in this troubled time by
being concerned with the questions of the prophets and
not the rote answers of the priests. For this task there
can be no easy solutions, nor single spokesmen, but rather
reaffirmation of those beliefs, goals, and responsibilities
among ourselves which once provided the fertile begin-
nings for the greatest prophets of Western civilization.
In this way we can teach ourselves and others the meaning of individual freedom, dignity, responsibility, and
peace.[7]

Jewish Messianism Is a Mission

For my generation, therefore, messianism has largely
come to mean a mission, a messiahship in which each Jew
must imitate the patriarchs and prophets, in which he is
responsible not only for the deliverance of the Jews but
also for the perfection of the world . . .[8]

Messianism Is at the Center of Jewish Uniqueness

Anyone who does not realize that the messianic vision
of redemption is central to the uniqueness of our people,
does not realize the basic truth of Jewish history and the
cornerstone of the Jewish faith . . . In the Messianic vision of redemption an organic bond was woven between
Jewish national redemption and general human redemption. The inner necessity of this combination will be
fully understood in our own days. In this generation,

[7]Marcus G. Raskin, in *Commentary* (New York), April, 1961.
[8]Irving Feldman, in *Commentary* (New York), April, 1961.

more than at any other previous period in the history of mankind, nations are interpendent, and even the mightiest of nations cannot safeguard its sovereignty, security and peace without bonds with other nations . . . The redemption of our people, therefore, is impossible, and its peace and security cannot be safeguarded, without the redemption of the world as a whole, without the achievement of general international peace, and unless peace and equality are established between the nations.[9]

Messiah Will Bring a New Divine Revelation

The Holy One handed down His Law through Divine Revelation, and it was only at our own request that He transmitted the remainder of the Torah through Moses. No one, no matter who he be, can be believed if he proclaims that he has been sent to add to, or detract from, what was given. But this does not oppose the belief that in the Messianic era we shall witness Divine Revelation once again. We believe that implicitly as Zechariah said: "Behold thy King cometh unto thee, he is just and bears deliverance; lowly, and riding upon an ass, even upon a colt, the foal of an ass" (9:9). Close upon that Zechariah adds: "And Jehovah shall be seen over them, and His arrow shall go forth as the lightning; and the Lord Jehovah will blow the horn, and will go with whirlwinds of the south."

Apart from the explicit words "And Jehovah shall be seen over them," the prophet clearly compares the attendant phenomena of this Divine Revelation with that great, eternal event of Divine Revelation on Mount Sinai. Apart from this distinct vision, other prophets hinted at a second Divine Revelation. One might have explained away those hints, were it not for the clear and distinct prophecy of Zechariah. This compels us to regard them

[9]David Ben-Gurion, "Vision and Redemption," *Forum for the Problems of Zionism, World Jewry and the State of Israel* (1959), Vol. 4, p. 113.

all as having but one meaning. When, for instance, Jeremiah prophesied as to a new covenant (31:31 ff.), he cannot be said to have had in mind the work of a prophet, for he contrasts the new covenant with the one made at Horeb. We have already quoted Isaiah and Micah: "And it shall come to pass in the end of days that the mountain of the Lord's house shall be established at the top of the mountains . . ." This cannot be said to mean that the nations of the world will receive instruction and guidance from one of the prophets of Israel. This is to be the greatest revolution in the history of the universe. And just as God brought His people, Israel, the loftiest and most soul-shaking revolution hitherto through revelation on Mount Sinai, we learn from the words of Zechariah and from the hints of Jeremiah, Isaiah and Micah that the nations of the world, together with Israel, will in the future be granted that lofty and stirring phenomenon of Divine Revelation. Hence, in those days, the nations which draw near to God will become substantially changed . . .

Let every man in Israel strengthen himself and encourage his friends and associates; let us mend our ways. Once more let us take upon ourselves the yoke of the Kingdom of Heaven and the yoke of the commandments. Let us fulfill our mission and work for the perfection of the world. If we shall do this we shall be worthy of witnessing our complete redemption and the advent of the Messiah, who will come and redeem us. May it be speedily in our own days![10]

"A Strange Factor in World Affairs"

Under the above caption a remarkable statement, reprinted below, appeared in *The Weekly Review* of August

[10]Aron Barth, *The Modern Jew Faces Eternal Problems* (Jersualem: The Religious Section of the Youth and Hechalutz Department of the Zionist Organization, 1956), pp. 227-228, 231. Used by permission.

26, 1960. *The Weekly Review* is not a religious publication. It is a news digest printed in England, and represents "a summary of political and economic intelligence for business men and advanced students of world affairs." This news service was started in December, 1938. It "is widely circulated to business executives and is subscribed to by official agencies of every important Government in the world, universities, Defence Colleges, and other institutions."

Amongst the strange signs of our times, none is more significant than the evolution of Israeli thinking about world affairs.

Drawn from all parts of the globe, the Jews in Palestine are in the most vulnerable military position imaginable. Many (though by no means all) have abandoned comfort and security elsewhere to place themselves in a position of extreme danger.

This extraordinary adventure has been backed by the financial aid of a community generally inclined to think more of profit than a mad adventure. Israel is the outstanding phenomenon of our times.

One detects amongst the Israel Jews a growing number of people who are developing a kind of exultation. Indeed there is a growing sense of a prophetic mission. More and more Israel Jews now see themselves as fulfilling ancient Biblical prophecies. More and more Jews in Palestine believe that no matter what the military odds may be Israel is fore-ordained to both the inevitability of battle and victory.

There are, of course, very many who hold no such opinions. Agnosticism and down to earth considerations remain widespread—but nothing like as widespread as ten years ago. The overall trend is towards belief in a prophetic mission and Divine protection.

Influence on Policy

This is very important because it influences policy. These beliefs make many influential Jews far more ready to face unpleasant facts in a way which we in Europe and America would not dream of. We are without any sense of special protection and fear of war makes us exclude it from our thinking to a large extent.

In Israel where the conviction of war, protection, and actual victory is now so widespread there is a growing tendency actually to look for signs of a coming conflict rather than as in the West to do the opposite.

Our observers have been much struck by this. We find in Israel an outlook totally different from that anywhere else to be seen. Many in Israel are convinced of four things which we in the West cannot bear to consider or if we do largely disbelieve.

Israel believes in (i) the certainty of war; (ii) the certainty of victory; (iii) protection from the popularly envisaged consequences of nuclear war; and (iv) a future order of society under actual Divine rule—a Messianic era.

An Unique Attitude

Indeed it is perhaps true to say that a new thinking has grown up in this strange country which is totally at variance with western thinking. If religious thinking in Europe and America is largely ethical, in Israel it tends more and more to belief in actual supernaturalism. This is the kind of belief which Moses had—that is to say belief in the actuality of Divine intervention in worldly affairs, totally upsetting the calculations and physical powers of a secular state.

A large part of Israel deeply and sincerely believes that world events are not finally decided by men. We face in this small country an opinion which is actually Biblical and we know of no other country where policy is influenced by a mystical concept regardless of any human or physical factor whatsoever.

It is partly because of this that either the Arab continent or Russia must back down or there must be a clash. The opinion held in Israel being as we have described, Israel herself will never do so. No Government in Israel could do so even if it so wished. If Communism is a driving force, Zionism in its present form is a far, far greater one. It is the only one of its kind on the side of the West. We may agree or disagree with it—but its exultation is absolute and forms an influence in world affairs which may prove of the greatest possible significance.

Israel believes that her testing time lies not far ahead, and expects that when it comes, regardless of how powerful Russia may be or what alliances she may have, an actual intervention by God will destroy every human calculation and Israel will be saved.

The Promised Land

Not only is this believed, but a growing number of Palestinian Jews believe that they will finally inherit the whole of the original area of the Promised Land and will be supreme in world affairs as the leaders of world religious and cultural thought. Many believe that this will occur as the result of the coming of a personal Messiah who will not only make Israel the world's leading nation, but will be the true physical descendant of King David.

That such views should emerge from an immigration largely agnostic in origins is a striking fact of which we in the West have far too little knowledge. Too little because it is a conviction of very great influence on policy in a vital area.[11]

[11]*The Weekly Review* (Buckinghamshire, England: The Weekly Review Ltd.) August 26, 1960. Used by permission.

The resumption of political independence by the Jewish people after a lapse of over two thousand years, and the growing conviction of many in the State of Israel that world history is pushing Israel nearer and nearer to the day when Israel must assume her divinely appointed mission, are matters of extreme importance to the Christian Church. The establishment of the kingdom of God on earth is the burden of the message of The Old Testament, and that it is also the burden of the message of the New Testament no objective person will deny. The petition "Thy kingdom come, thy will be done on earth as in heaven" was inserted by Jesus at the very beginning of the "Lord's Prayer" and has been recited by countless generations of Christians for nineteen centuries. Thus present-day world events, under the overruling guidance of the God of history, have created a common meeting ground for both the Jewish people and the Church of Jesus Christ. Never before in the entire Christian era did exactly this kind of an opportunity exist. May all true Jews and true Christians work and pray that neither Israel nor the Christian Church shall let this day of opportunity pass.

IV. THE HEBREW CHRISTIAN MISSION

The modern Hebrew-Christian movement is about a hundred years old. Its origin coincides in time with the national reawakening of the Jewish people in the nineteenth century. Its separate and distinctive existence is marked by a deep consciousness of its kinship with the Jewish people and an awareness of the unique character of its mission. Its mission is to maintain in the midst of the Jewish people a candlestick of witness of the messiahship of Jesus.

The reader's attention is invited again to a statement, referred to previously in this study, from a work in which the author—an eminent religious Israel Jew—cites passages from the prophetic writings of the Old Testament to prove that the Old Testament teaches that there will be a new divine revelation in the messianic era. This is a significant departure from the position taken in certain rabbinic writings and the Maimonides Creed—aimed to disprove the truth of Christianity—that the Law of Moses is God's last word to man. The same writer also states that the new revelation which Israel will receive in the messianic era will be of the same epoch-making character as the Mount Sinai revelation and will constitute "the greatest revolution in the history of the universe."

We find in the Biblical record that God often prepares those to whom He is about to vouchsafe His truth. He does this at times directly, at other times indirectly through historical events, but frequently utilizing both methods. Israel has been prepared for the Sinai revelation by the bondage in Egypt and through the existence among the Hebrews in Egypt of a tradition of certain divine promises received by Abraham.

There is every reason to believe that Israel will be similarly prepared for the new revelation to come in the messianic era. This preparation will also consist of two elements: (1) world events operating from the outside, and (2) the existence of a faithful testimony in the midst of Israel. To be that testimony within Israel is the function of present-day Hebrew Christianity. Our task is to help the Jewish people recover faith in a personal God, faith in the Bible as the Word of God, and faith in a personal Messiah as the Redeemer of Israel and the Saviour of the world. Our mission is to be heralds of the coming redemption, and voices crying, "Prepare ye in the wilderness a way for Jehovah, make level in the desert a highway for our God."

V. A DAY OF OPPORTUNITY FOR THE CHRISTIAN CHURCH

For the first time since the Protestant Reformation the bulk of the Jewish people live in countries of Protestant Christendom. There is evidence that certain Jews are impressed by the relevance of the theological thinking which prevails in certain segments of Protestant Christianity, as seen from the following excerpts.

In this age of longing, Jewish students and intellectuals often seek Jewish authenticity on a Protestant model. They read thinkers such as Buber and Heschel, who play the same role that Niebuhr and Tillich play in Protestant circles, namely, that of mediators of the traditional faith to modern man. I myself have traveled this way. In a period of estrangement from Judaism, I was deeply impressed by the intellectual vitality of contemporary Protestant thinkers and, in studying them, I was directed to the creative Jewish thinkers of our time, especially to Martin Buber, who helped me along the road to a reaffirmation of Judaism.[12]

Another Jewish observer finds certain crucial Jewish insights illumined when viewed in the light shed on them by Christian doctrine.[13]

The writer of the following lines acknowledges that certain Christian writings helped him gain a better understanding of Judaism.

[12]Malcolm L. Diamond, in *Commentary* (New York), April, 1961.
[13]Will Herberg, "From Marxism to Judaism," *Commentary* (New York), January, 1947.

Decisive in my present Jewish engagements are my friendship since 1944 with Professor Abraham Joshua Heschel of the Jewish Theological Seminary and my dialogue over the last seventeen years with the thought and person of Martin Buber . . . I should mention, finally, my dialogue over many years with a wide range of Christian thinkers and Christian thought . . . Through this dialogue as also through the dialogue with the other great world religions that I have for many years studied and taught, the central place of Judaism in my thought and attitudes has become ever clearer to me.[14]

Of even greater significance is the total effect of the Christian way of life upon the Jewish population.

Normally, I suppose, I haven't any attitude toward my own Jewishness, because normally I'm not aware of it. The question seems to me to be this: on what sorts of occasions is one made aware of it. I say "made aware of it" rather than "become aware of it" because for those of us whose parents were born in America, and whose homes are in no profound way touched by Jewishness . . . for those of us, that is, whose parents had already rebelled against the Orthodox traditions before we were born, there is nothing in being Jewish which is present in us in daily life as a matter of course. A cue from outside is necessary to remind us of it. And for many quite obvious reasons, there are fewer jolts and shocks from outside than there were fifteen to twenty years ago.

But while the cues no longer come in the violent form they took then, no Jew living in a society as saturated with the forms and language of Christianity as America is can fail from time to time to be reminded of the fact that he is a Jew. One doesn't fear anti-Semitism, one doesn't in fact fear anything at all—but one is reminded: when political conventions are opened with a prayer,

[14]Maurice Friedman, in *Judaism* (New York), Fall, 1961.

when one meets the expressions "Christian country" and "Jewish vote," when hymns are sung at the opening or closing of meetings whose purpose is totally non-religious. In fact, anything that smacks of religion at all will do the trick.

Of course no one intends anti-Semitism, nor do I take these reminders as anti-Semitic. The hymns are chosen with care, and no one could possibly take offense . . .

But the curious thing is that these things should remind us of being Jewish. I think the reason lies in just the sort of non-religious background I mentioned . . .

One is, in America, very often reminded of religion, and of the existence of those for whom belief has a role to play, or at least of those for whom it appears to have a role to play.[15]

Concluding Remarks

Israel is a remarkable people. Its history, perhaps more than the history of any other nation, is a demonstration of the working out of God's faithfulness. If the Christian Church will remain loyal to its divine Master, true to its confession, and faithful to its commission, the Jew will continue to be reminded of his Jewishness, as long as Jewishness will be what it has come to be, a way of life from which God is left out. But the Church must do more than this. She needs to search her heart and see in what areas she has failed in relation to Israel. She needs to stretch out her hand to Israel and, in a fresh outpouring of Christian love, seek for ways of a possible reconciliation. Then she may hasten the dawn of the day when Israel as a nation shall return to Jehovah and to its spiritual heritage. For the coming of that day many of the remnant of Israel are praying, a world in dire need is hoping, and a loving and long-suffering God is waiting.

[15]Judith Jarvis, in *Commentary* (New York), April, 1961.

CHAPTER 11

ISRAEL AT THE END-TIME

OF HISTORY

THE INDESTRUCTIBILITY OF ISRAEL—A PERMANENT AND FULL
RESTORATION OF ISRAEL IS PREDICTED IN THE BIBLE—THE
PERMANENT RESTORATION OF ISRAEL WILL COINCIDE WITH THE
ADVENT OF THE MESSIAH—ISRAEL'S RESTORATION ACCORDING
TO THE NEW TESTAMENT

I. THE INDESTRUCTIBILITY OF ISRAEL

IN A.D. 66 the Jews of the land of Israel rose in rebellion against
the Romans, who had occupied the land since the first century
B.C. The struggle against the Romans, bitter and protracted,
ended with the destruction of Jerusalem and the Second Temple in A.D. 70. In 132 another attempt was made by the Jews
to throw off the Roman yoke. It was terminated in A.D. 135
with the destruction of the Land of Israel and the dispersion
of the Jews. There is a large body of Biblical writings which
assumes the existence of an independent Jewish state in the
Land of Israel at the end-time of history. This can mean one
thing only, namely, that some time before the return of Jesus
Christ the Jews will reconstitute their nationhood in the Land
of Israel.[1]

The following Scripture citations show that though Israel
may be dispossessed of her God-given land, she will never be
destroyed.

Yet for all that, when they are in the land of their enemies,

[1]For a detailed study of this subject, see my book *The Rebirth of the
State of Israel* and a companion volume *The Death and Resurrection of
Israel*.

I will not spurn them, neither will I abhor them so as to destroy them utterly and break my covenant with them; for I am the LORD their God; but I will for their sake remember the covenant with their forefathers, whom I brought forth out of the land of Egypt in the sight of the nations, that I might be their God: I am the LORD.

Leviticus 26:44-45

Behold, the eyes of the Lord God are upon the sinful kingdom [of Israel], and I will destroy it from the surface of the ground; except that I will not utterly destroy the house of Jacob, says the LORD.

Amos 9:8

For I am with you to save you, says the LORD; I will make a full end of all the nations among whom I scattered you, but of you I will not make a full end. I will chasten you in just measure, and I will by no means leave you unpunished.

Jeremiah 30:11

Thus says the LORD, who gives the sun for light by day and the fixed order of the moon and the stars for light by night, who stirs up the sea so that its waves roar—the LORD of hosts is his name: "If this fixed order departs from before me, says the LORD, then shall the descendants of Israel cease from being a nation before me for ever." Thus says the LORD: "If the heavens above can be measured, and the foundations of the earth below can be explored, then I will cast off all the descendants of Israel for all that they have done, says the LORD."

Jeremiah 31:35-37

II. A PERMANENT AND FULL RESTORATION OF ISRAEL IS PREDICTED IN THE BIBLE

The passages cited below predict a *permanent* restoration of Israel and the Davidic dynasty.

In that day I will raise up the booth [tabernacle] of David[2] that is fallen and repair its breaches, and raise up its ruins, and rebuild it as in the days of old. . . . I will restore the fortunes of my people Israel, and they shall rebuild the ruined cities and inhabit them; they shall plant vineyards and drink their wine, and they shall make gardens and eat their fruit. I will plant them upon their land, and they shall never again be plucked up out of the land which I have given them, says the LORD your God.

Amos 9:11, 14-15

Thus says the Lord GOD: Behold, I will take the people of Israel from the nations among which they have gone, and will gather them from all sides, and bring them to their own land; and I will make them one nation in the land, upon the mountains of Israel; and one king shall be king over them all; and they shall be no longer two nations, and no longer divided into two kingdoms.[3] They shall not defile themselves any more with their idols and their detestable things, or with any of their transgressions; but I will save them from all the backslidings in which they have sinned, and will cleanse them; and they shall be my people, and I will be their God.

My servant David shall be king over them; and they shall all have one shepherd. They shall follow my ordinances and be careful to observe my statutes. They shall dwell in the land where your fathers dwelt that I gave to my servant Jacob; they and their children and their children's children shall dwell there for ever; and David my servant shall be their prince for ever. I will make a covenant of peace with them; it shall be an everlasting covenant with them; and I will bless them and multiply them, and will set my sanctuary in the midst of them for evermore. My dwelling place shall be with them; and I will be their God, and they shall be my people. Then the nations will know

[2]The Davidic dynasty.
[3]This refers to the secession of the northern tribes from the Davidic dynasty, resulting in a division of Israel into two states.

that I the LORD sanctify Israel, when my sanctuary is in the midst of them for evermore.

Ezekiel 37:21-28

III. THE PERMANENT RESTORATION OF ISRAEL WILL COINCIDE WITH THE ADVENT OF THE MESSIAH

1. The Messianic Prophecies of Isaiah

It is generally agreed by Bible scholars, both Jewish and Christian, that the message in Isaiah 11 and 12 is one of the great messianic utterances in the Old Testament. We will cite only a few excerpts. In the opening portion of his message Isaiah declares indirectly that the Messiah will come some time *after* the extinction of the Davidic dynasty, even though the Davidic dynasty will last approximately 150 years following this prophecy.

There shall come forth a shoot from the stump of Jesse,[4] and a branch shall grow out of his roots. And the Spirit of the LORD shall rest upon him, the spirit of wisdom and understanding, the spirit of counsel and might, the spirit of knowledge and the fear of the LORD. And his delight shall be in the fear of the LORD.

He shall not judge by what his eyes see, or decide by what his ears hear; but with righteousness he shall judge the poor, and decide with equity for the meek of the earth; and he shall smite the earth with the rod of his mouth, and with the breath of his lips he shall slay the wicked. Righteousness shall be the girdle of his waist, and faithfulness the girdle of his loins.

Isaiah 11:1-5

---

[4]Jesse, David's father, is specified here rather than David, probably to emphasize the fact that there will be no Davidic dynasty in existence at the time of the Messiah's advent.

In the passage that follows the prophet predicts a second ingathering of Israel, from its worldwide dispersion.

> In that day the LORD will extend his hand yet a second time to recover the remnant which is left of his people from Assyria, from Egypt, from Pathros, from Ethiopia, from Elam, from Shinar, from Hamath, and from the coastlands of the sea. He will raise an ensign [banner] for the nations, and will assemble the outcasts of Israel, and gather the dispersed of Judah from the four corners of the earth.
>
> Isaiah 11:11-12

This ingathering will be from a *worldwide* dispersion: from the countries of the Middle East, and from the "coastlands of the sea," which is the Old Testament term for Europe. There was no such worldwide dispersion of the Jews in Isaiah's day. The Exodus from Egypt was not an ingathering of the remnant of Israel. The Jews went to Egypt voluntarily and few in number; there they became a nation. And the Exodus was from Egypt and only from Egypt. The *first* time an ingathering of a remnant of Jews from a wide dispersion occurred was at the end of the Babylonian exile. The ingathering predicted by Isaiah in chapter 11 is a *second* such ingathering.

Another interesting element about this predicted second ingathering is that the nations of the world will have a part in it, and the involvement of these nations will be directed by the Messiah (v. 12).

That the message of Isaiah 11 is messianic and destined for fulfillment at the end-time of history is indicated by the term "in that day," with which verses 10 and 11 begin. "In that day" is used by Isaiah in the same sense as he uses the phrase "in the latter days."

The short chapter 12 contains the song of praise and thanksgiving to be rendered by the returning remnant for God's gracious dealings with them.

You will say in that day: "I will give thanks to thee, O LORD, for though thou wast angry with me, thy anger turned away, and thou didst comfort me.

"Behold, God is my salvation; I will trust, and will not be afraid; for the LORD GOD is my strength and my song, and he has become my salvation."

With joy you will draw water from the wells of salvation. And you will say in that day: "Give thanks to the LORD, call upon his name; make known his deeds among the nations, proclaim that his name is exalted.

"Sing praises to the LORD, for he has done gloriously; let this be known in all the earth. Shout, and sing for joy, O inhabitant of Zion, for great in your midst is the Holy One of Israel."

Isaiah 12:1-6

2. The Messianic Prophecies of Hosea

For the children of Israel shall dwell many days without king or prince, without sacrifice or pillar, without ephod or teraphim. Afterward the children of Israel shall return and seek the LORD their God, and David their king; and they shall come in fear to the LORD and to his goodness in the latter days.

Hosea 3:4-5

The Period of Many Days *in Jewish History*

Hosea 3:4-5 is a prophetic forecast of two periods in Jewish history; first, a long period designated as the period of *many days;* second, a short period identified as the period of *latter days.* Israel's condition in the period of *many days* is described in verse 4. Politically, the Jews will be a people without a government of their own (a king or prince). Religiously, they will be without *sacrifice* and without *pillar*, without *ephod* or *teraphim*. *Sacrifice* stands here for the sacrificial system of the Sinai covenant; *pillar* represents the pagan religions which Israel frequently copied from her heathen neighbors. *Ephod* symbolizes the means of communicating with God as provided in the Sinai revelation; *teraphim* were pagan household deities which Israel's neighbors used to communicate with their gods.[5] In other words, during the period of *many days* Israel will be a people without a government of its own, and without the true religion of the Sinai covenant or even the false religion of paganism.

It is quite possible that Hosea understood the message recorded in Hosea 3:4-5 as applying to his beloved native northern kingdom of Israel. But the prophets knew only what God wished to communicate to them, and God revealed to them only what they needed to know and what they were capable of comprehending at the time the divine revelation was granted to them. The message of Hosea 3:4-5 was never fulfilled in the history of the northern kingdom of Israel, either in Hosea's day or at any time after Hosea. The Israel in Hosea 3:4-5 is not a pagan Israel, whereas the Israel of the northern kingdom was almost fully paganized. It was eventually destroyed by the Assyrians in 721 B.C., its people were deported to Assyria, and there they merged fully with their heathen neighbors.

The prophetic message of Hosea 3:4 entered upon its fulfillment in the events of Jewish history which began in A.D. 70, the period of the Great Dispersion of the Jews. The following is a comment on the "many days" period of the Hosea prophecy by Rabbi David Kimchi, one of the medieval Jewish Bible expositors.

> These are the days of the present exile, in which we are in the power of the Gentiles, and in the power of their kings and princes, and we are "without a sacrifice and without an image," i.e., without a sacrifice to God, and without an image to false gods; and without an ephod, and without teraphim, i.e., without an ephod to God, by means of which we could foretell the future, as with the Urim and Thummim; and without teraphim

[5] It is believed that the reason Rachel stole the teraphim of her pagan father Laban was to make it impossible for him to discover through the teraphim the direction in which Jacob's family fled.

to false gods. And this is the present condition of all the children of Israel in this present exile.

The Mosaic law of the Sinai Covenant knows of only one true religion, namely, the religion in the center of which stands the Levitical sacrifice. If in the period of the many days the Jewish people were to have neither the true religion of the Mosaic Law nor the false religion of idolatry, what religion, if any, were they to have during this long period of many days? From A.D. 70 to the period of political emancipation which came in the eighteenth century, during this period of some seventeen hundred years, the Jewish people were saturated with religion. During that period the Jews produced practically all of their Talmudic literature which became the basis of traditional Judaism.

Although the wheels of Biblical prophecy often grind slowly, they nonetheless grind surely. When in the wake of the French Revolution the ghetto walls of Jewish forced isolation were broken down in many countries of Western Europe and the Jews began to enter the mainstream of the life of the countries of their residence, they soon realized that their Talmudic Judaism was a religion fit for the restricted, abnormal life in the ghettos, but totally unsuitable for Jews living as full-fledged citizens of their countries. This unpleasant discovery some 150 years ago was the beginning of the disintegration of Talmudic or traditional Judaism, and in the course of time the Jews have been transformed into a people who are largely religiously indifferent, as seen from the following representative statements by leading Jewish spokesmen.

"We may still speak of ourselves as a religious people," said Nathan A. Barak. "The fact is we no longer are. Many of us look back nostalgically to our religious days: our longing will not restore them. There can be no religion without faith and feeling. We lack both elements. Today, most Jews are no longer able to pray. . . . One prays to God not by addressing him verbally. One must know in one's heart to whom he prays. We do not."[6]

In an article entitled "Has Judaism Still Power to Speak?" Will Herberg said that not even the Nazi catastrophe generated any sign of a religious awakening among the Jews. "We have long prided ourselves," he said, "as being the universally recognized People of the Book. What have we done to make the Book relevant to the perplexities of our age? What has been our response in terms of creative religious thinking, theological interpretation or prophetic witness? What word has Judaism for mankind in agony?"[7] The implied answer is: None!

Referring to the absence of genuine religious experience among the Jews, one Jewish observer said: "I think I do not exaggerate when I say there is nothing in American Jewish literature . . . that might possibly find a place in any anthology of religious experience. I once asked one of our leading authorities on American Jewish history whether he knew of any autobiography . . . by rabbi or layman that described in detail a spiritual or religious experience. He could think only of the autobiography of a Jew who had been converted to Christianity."[8]

Hosea's words describe just such a situation: "For the children of Israel shall dwell many days without king or prince, without sacrifice or pillar, without ephod or teraphim [i.e., without true religion or false religion]."

[6]Rabbi Nathan A. Barak, "War and the Spirit of Israel," *Contemporary Jewish Record* (now *Commentary*, New York), August 1942.
[7]Will Herberg, "Has Judaism Still Power to Speak?" *Commentary* (New York), May 1949.
[8]Nathan Glazer, "The Jewish Revival in America," II, *Commentary* (New York), May 1949.

The Period of Latter Days

With the end of the period of Jewish history identified by Hosea as the period of *many days*, a new period of Jewish history will begin, the period of *latter days*.

> Afterward the people of Israel shall return and seek the LORD their God, and David their king; and they shall come in fear to the LORD and to his goodness in the latter days.
>
> Hosea 3:5

"Afterward," i.e., after the period of *many days* has run its course, the period of *latter days* will begin. Whatever else the phrase "latter days" may mean in the Bible, it always suggests the end-time of history ushered in by the coming of the Messiah. Moreover, in the Hosea prophecy the advent of the Messiah is specifically indicated by the words "David their king." We are told in the Hosea passage that when the period of *many days* will have terminated, the Jewish people will seek "Jehovah their God and David their king."

But "David their king" cannot refer to King David, who had been dead over two hundred years when Hosea delivered his prophetic message. It cannot suggest the Davidic dynasty, since the royal house of David came to an end with Zedekiah, the last Davidic king, and the Davidic dynasty was not to be restored until the Messiah would come.[9] Consequently, Jewish Bible expositors are correct when they interpret this "David their king" statement as referring to King Messiah who has to be a descendant of the royal house of David.

In the period of the *latter days* the Jewish people will turn and seek Jehovah their God and their messianic king. The Hebrew word which is translated "turn" in the English Bible is related to a word which means *repent* or *repentance*. Thus in

---

[9]See Isaiah 9:6-7 (9:5-6 Heb.); 11:1-12; Jeremiah 23:5-6; Ezekiel 21:25-27 (21:30-32 Heb.). See especially Rabbi Dr. S. Fisch's comment on the Ezekiel passage in *Ezekiel* (The Soncino Press: London, 1950), pp. 140-141.

this period Israel will turn in repentance to their God and to their messianic king, from whom they had been alienated in the *many days* period. Notice that they will simultaneously turn to God and to the Messiah, which event will accomplish their spiritual rebirth and their full national restoration.

Israel's Spiritual Rebirth and Permanent and Full National Restoration Will Take Place in a Time of Trouble

> And they shall come in fear [trembling] to the LORD and to his goodness in the latter days.
>
> Hosea 3:5b

There are two passages in Hosea which explain the meaning of the above statement. One is found in Hosea 5:15:

> I will return again to my place, until they acknowledge their guilt and seek my face, and in their distress they seek me. . . .

During the period of *many days* God will have withdrawn His holy presence from Israel, until in their trouble they acknowledge their guilt and seek God in repentance.

A second passage which sheds additional light on the idea of fear or trembling in Hosea 3:5b follows. Describing the return of the Jewish people from the various places of their dispersion to the Land of Israel, God declares:

> They shall go after the LORD, he will roar like a lion; yea, he will roar, and his sons shall come trembling from the west; they shall come trembling like birds from Egypt, and like doves from the land of Assyria; and I will return them to their homes, says the LORD.
>
> Hosea 11:10-11

It will be a time of affliction when the Jewish people return to the Land of Israel. It will be a time of affliction when the Jews will return to God in repentance—a time of trouble for Israel, and affliction for the world at large. Has not this prophecy been at least partly fulfilled when in the wake of the Holocaust many Jews, broken in body and spirit, began to pour into the Land of Israel from the east and the west?

In 1948 the Jewish people resumed their national existence in the Land of Israel. With the exception of the Jews living in Soviet Russia, most Jews who now desire to live under a Jewish government are free to do so by resettling in the Land of Israel. Shall we then say that in one respect the period of *many days* has come to an end, or is drawing to an end? And if so, is there any indication of a turning to God and a turning to the messianic king on the part of the Jewish people of today?

We are told that in the last ten years thousands of young Jews have acknowledged Jesus as the promised Messiah and as their Lord and Savior. Many of these Jews have been delivered from the hell of drugs and other evils through their spiritual conversion which resulted from a confrontation with the message of the Gospel. What about the Jews in the Land of Israel? In 1969 a book entitled *Israel: The Sword And The Harp* was published. The writer, a British Jew, spent five years as a visiting professor in two universities in Israel. A whole chapter in this book under the title, "The Figure of Jesus on the Israeli Horizon," is devoted to the subject of Jesus. The following is an excerpt from that chapter.

> The figure of Jesus, the Jew from Nazareth, looms large on the Israeli horizon, although not much is said about him openly, and most Jews cautiously refrain from mentioning his name in public. Still, he is very much in the mind of the Israeli Jews, more now than ever, and the awareness of his shadow is growing. In the Galilee, the most beautiful and inspiring part of Israel, he is the dominating figure. Every site of antiquity and

every beauty spot in Galilee bears his footprints. He is still 'walking' by the sea of Galilee (Matthew 4:18); on the Sabbath day he enters into the Synagogue in Capernaum (Mark 1:21); in Tabgha, close to Capernaum, he performs the miracle of the loaves and fishes (Luke 11:17). On the Mount of Beatitudes which overlooks the waters of the Lake[10] he utters his immortal Sermon on the Mount. Of course, Nazareth is the center of his life, and Jerusalem the scene of his last ministry. Much of the charm and magnetism of the holy land is due, not only to the echoes of the Bible, but also to the echoes of Jesus' life. . . .

The mystery of this simple Jew from Nazareth, who managed to conquer almost the whole world and whose spiritual power was stronger than that of the whole of Jewry, is simply puzzling to the Israeli Jew. Who was he? Where lies the secret and mystery of his power? How did this Jew manage to attract the immense love and adoration of the world, while the Jews attracted only hatred and contempt? How did he manage to fulfill the task set in the Bible for the Jews to serve as 'a light unto the nations', while Jewry failed? Why was it that only he managed to shape and mould the world, while the Jews played a losing game, rolling in the dust? Why has the genius of Jesus never been repeated within the Jewish gates? And will it ever be repeated? . . .

The tragedy of Israel is that the old religion, practised only by the orthodox, is ritualistic, petrified and ossified, and deprived of its vivifying, life-enhancing and tender forces, while the rest of society, the majority, is atheistic, agnostic or religiously indifferent, disinterested or unconcerned. So religion in Israel is hardly alive in any direction. . . . Could it be that Jesus could give it a new lease of life?[11]

Some idea of the unusual interest in Jesus among the Jews in the State of Israel may be gained from the following: Since

[10]The Biblical Sea of Galilee.
[11]Ferdynand Zweig, *Israel: The Sword and the Harp* (Cranbury, N.J.: Fairleigh Dickinson University Press, 1969), pp. 219, 225-6, 228, 229. Used by permission.
[12]"How Jews See Jews," *Newsweek*, April 18, 1977, p. 88.

the re-establishment of the State of Israel in 1948 over 187 books, essays, poems, and articles and 233 other works—all about Jesus—have been produced by Israeli authors.[12]

According to Pinchas Lapide, an Orthodox Israeli Jew and former chairman of the Department of Applied Linguistics at Bar-Ilan University of Israel, the twenty-nine Hebrew books on Jesus published in recent years "have in common a sympathy and a love for the Nazarene which would have been impossible at any other time during the past eighteen hundred years."[13]

> For the children of Israel shall dwell many days without king or prince, without sacrifice or pillar, without ephod or teraphim. Afterward the children of Israel shall return and seek the LORD their God, and David their king; and they shall come in fear to the LORD and to his goodness in the latter days.

IV. ISRAEL'S RESTORATION ACCORDING TO THE NEW TESTAMENT

> Jesus said to them [the apostles], "Truly I say to you, that you who have followed Me, in the regeneration[14] when the Son of Man will sit on His glorious throne, you also shall sit upon twelve thrones, judging the twelve tribes of Israel."
>
> Matthew 14:28 (NASB)

> And you are those who have stood by me in my trials; and just as My Father has granted Me a kingdom I grant you that you may eat and drink at My table in My kingdom, and you will sit on thrones judging the twelve tribes of Israel.
>
> Luke 22:28-30 (NASB)

[13]Pinchas E. Lapide, *Is This Joseph's Son?* quoted in Hans Küng, *Signposts for the Future*, trans. Edward Quinn (Garden City, N.Y.: Doubleday, 1977, 1978), p. 71.
[14]Regeneration—a term used to describe the purification and rejuvenation of the earth brought about by the upheavals accompanying the return of Jesus.

Following His resurrection the risen Jesus appeared to the disciples, off and on, in the space of forty days.

> And while staying with them he charged them not to depart from Jerusalem, but to wait for the promise of the Father, which, he said, "you heard from me, for John [John the Baptizer] baptized with water, but before many days you shall be baptized with the Holy Spirit."
> So when they had come together, they asked him, "Lord, will you at this time restore the kingdom to Israel?" He said to them, "It is not for you to know times or seasons which the Father has fixed by his own authority. But you shall receive power when the Holy Spirit has come upon you; and you shall be my witnesses in Jerusalem and in all Judea and Samaria and to the end of the earth." And when he had said this, as they were looking on, he was lifted up, and a cloud took him out of their sight.
>
> Acts 1:4-9

Commenting on the above passage in the book of Acts, Robert D. Culver says:

> For forty days the Lord, intermittently of course, explained to the disciples the "kingdom of God." This He did to men whose minds were steeped in the Old Testament promises to Israel in connection with that kingdom. It were vain, of course, to suppose that the bearings of that kingdom on the present age were not discussed—but the fact remains that after forty days of this instruction the Jewish disciples still believed that some time in the future the kingdom would be restored to them. Jesus did not tell them that their hope was false. He did not reprove them for a "carnal" view of the kingdom. He informed them only that it was not for them to know the time at which the restoration would take place.[15]

[15]Robert D. Culver, *Daniel and the Latter Days* (Westwood, N.J.: Fleming H. Revell Co., 1954), pp. 84-85.

Lest you be wise in your own conceits, I want you to understand this mystery, brethren: a hardening has come upon part of Israel, until the full number of the Gentiles come in, and so all Israel will be saved; as it is written, "The Deliverer will come from Zion, he will banish ungodliness from Jacob"; "and this will be my covenant with them when I take away their sins."

Romans 11:25-27

The following exposition of the context of the above passage is by the late Alva J. McClain, president of Grace College and president and professor of Grace Theological Seminary.

Is He, God, done with Israel as a nation? The apostle recoils from such a suggestion, and proceeds to show that the rejection of Israel is even now not total, but only partial. And even this partial rejection is not final, but only temporary. Three facts are advanced to prove that God has not cast off His people forever. First, there is a PRESENT ELECTION within the nation (Romans 11:1-10). He has spoken of this before, but he now points to himself, an Israelite among the saved, as an evidence to this election. Furthermore, the existing situation is very similar to that in the days of Elijah when in the whole nation there was but a small remnant who had not bowed the knee to Baal. So now there is a remnant according to the election of grace. As to the rest, they have been hardened, and their eyes darkened. Nevertheless, we are not to suppose that this is the end of Israel's national hopes. There is to be a FUTURE RESTORATION of the nation back to the divine favor (Romans 11:11-24). Israel did not stumble that he might fall irretrievably. There was a beneficent purpose in permitting all this to take place. Through the fall of Israel great riches have been brought to the Gentile world, and if his fall meant much to the world, certainly his future reception back into favor will mean much more. If, on account of unbelief, certain Israelite branches have been broken off out of the tree of God's favor and Gentile branches have been grafted in, we are not to forget that God is able to graft the Israelite back into the place of favor. For, after all, they are the natural branches; God's favor came into the world through Israel. As a matter of fact, they shall be grafted again into their own tree. There is to be a final SALVATION for the nation[16] (Romans 11:25-32).

[16]Alva J. McClain, *Romans Outlined and Summarized*, pp. 36, 37; cited in Culver, Op. Cit., pp. 85-86.

INDEX